Corrective Reading

Workbook

SRA Word-Attack Basics

Decoding A

Siegfried Engelmann
Linda Carnine
Gary Johnson

SRA

Columbus, OH

SRAonline.com

Printed in the United States of America.

Send all inquiries to this address:
SRA/McGraw-Hill
4400 Easton Commons
Columbus, OH 43219

ISBN: 978-0-07-611206-7
MHID: 0-07-611206-3

6 7 8 9 QPE 13 12 11 10 09

The McGraw·Hill Companies

A | B | C =

1

t a s e m

___ ___ ___ ___ ___ ___ ___ ___ ___ ___

2

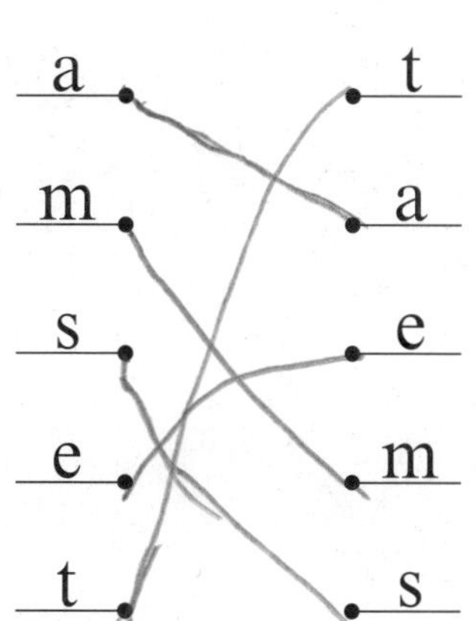

3

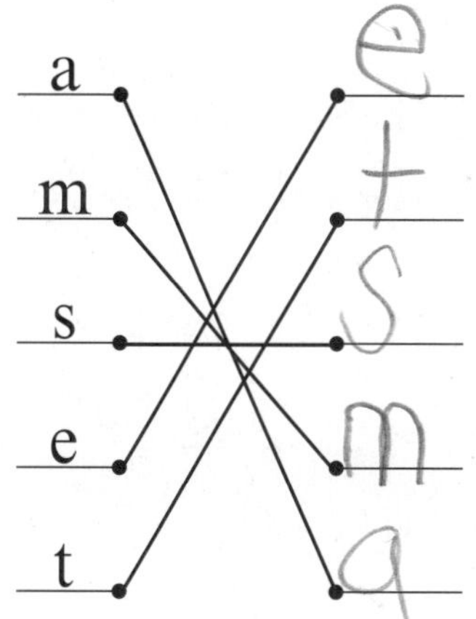

4

1. me 2. am 3. ma 4. eem

5

(m) m s a m t e s a m e t a m t s m e t a t m e s s a
s t e m a s m a t m s t a m s e t m e m s m e m (14)

(a) s t e m a t m e s t m e a s t m a m e s t t a s e t
m e s t m a t s a m e t a e m t e a m t a m e s a (10)

(t) s e m a s e a t a m e t a s e s e a e s a t e a s t
m s m e t m a m s m e m t a s t m a m s t e m s (8)

1

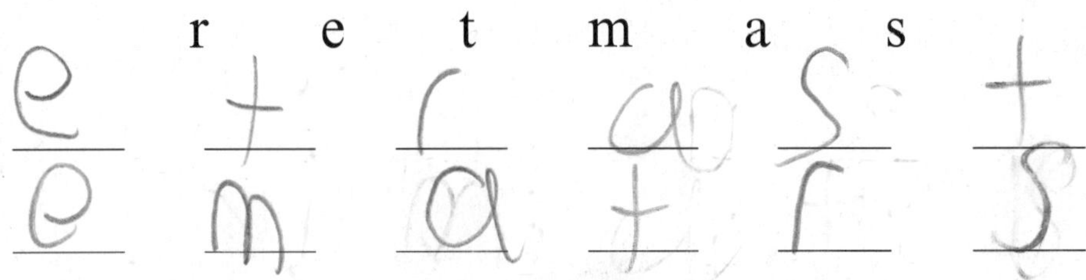

2

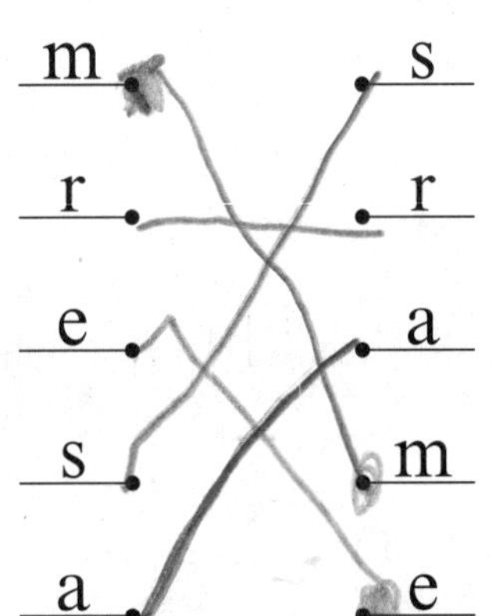

3

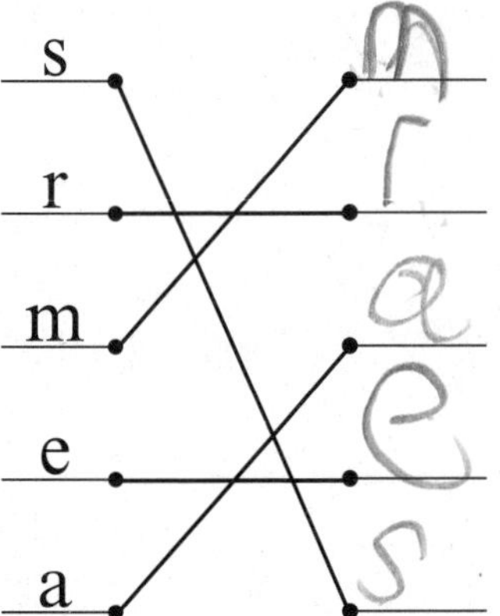

4

1. me 2. am 3. ree

4. see 5. eem 6. ma

5

(e) t r e s m a r t e m s a m e t r s r a t e m s a r e
s m e t a r e m t a s e m s a e m t m e s e a s e

(a) s t a r e m a s r a m e s e m a m e a t m e a s r
m s a r e r m s m a m e m s m r t a s e a r a m

(r) a s m e r t e s a t r e s e r t a m s e t m e s a a
r m e s e a m t e r a m s m e r a m t r e m a m s

A	B	C	=	
6	8	6	=	20

1

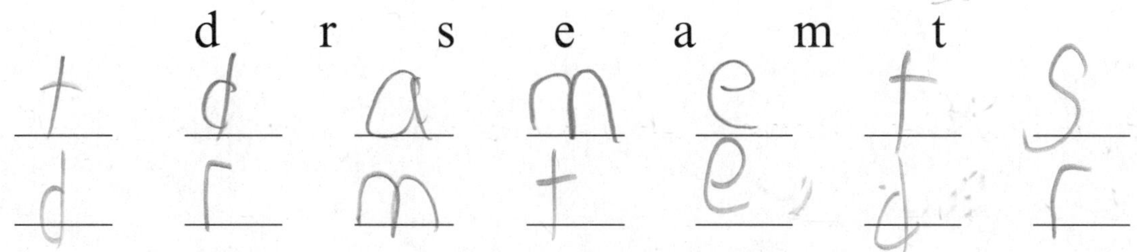

2

1. ra 2. sa 3. ees

4. ma 5. meet 6. see

3

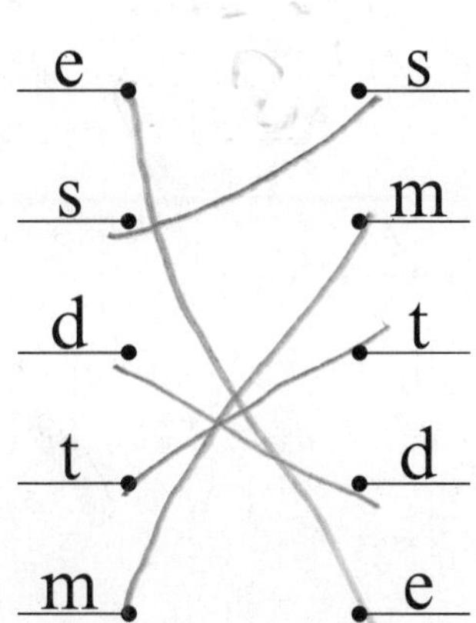

4

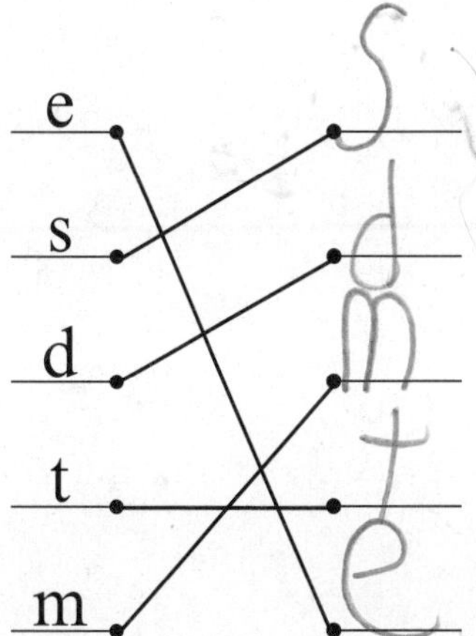

5

(d) e r s d m d r a e t r d m t r a s e d m e d t r a m
d s t r t r d t r m s d t r m r t d t s t d m e r s d (11)

(t) d t r a m d r t a d r t r m e r a r t r m a m t m e
m r a m e t r d e m t r d t r t d d t r e d t a m d (11)

(d) d t r a m d r t m a r a e s t r d e a d r t m t s d r t r
m d r t d m a r t r t d r t d m a r t r t d r a m d r t d (12)

Lesson 4

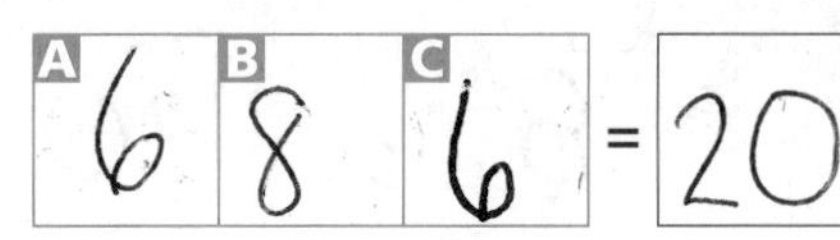

1

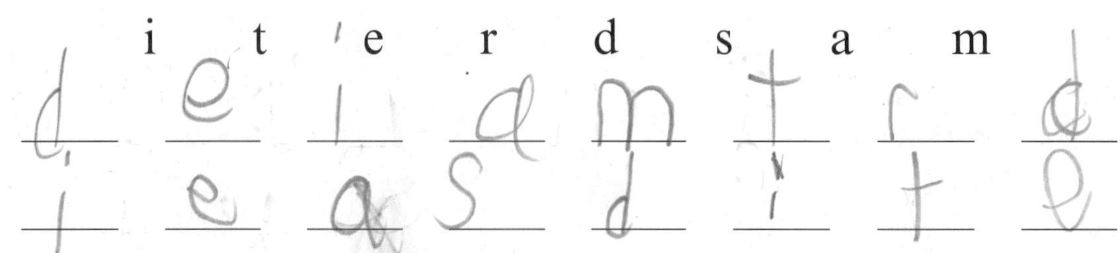

2

1. sa
2. sad
3. sat
4. mat
5. ees
6. me
7. at
8. am
9. ma

3

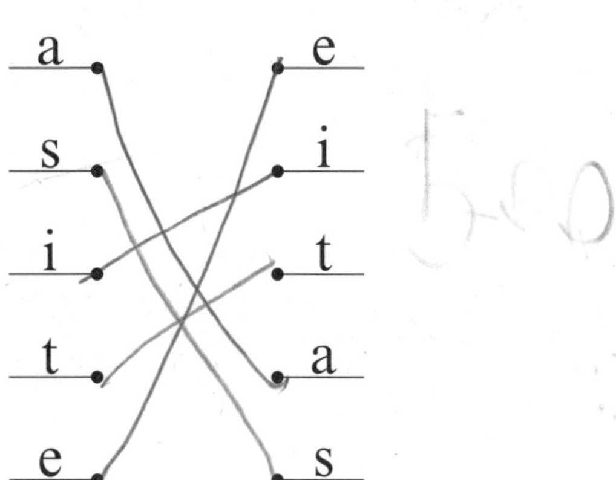

4

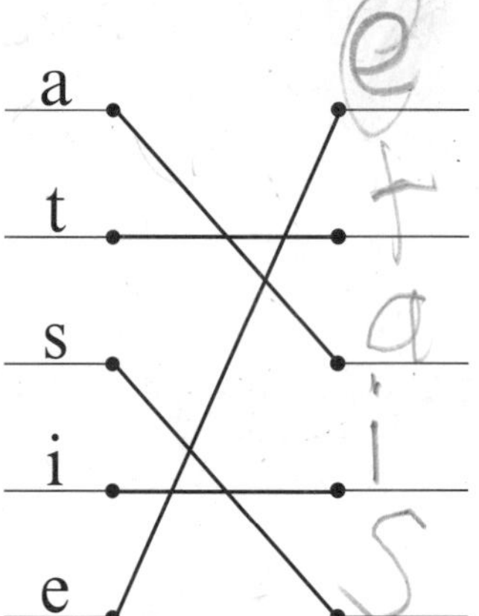

5

(i) m i s r e t i d r d i m a t i s d e m s a i t r d i e
a t s i t d i d m a t i s r a i e i r i s t m s r d t i (13)

(a) a r a m e a m t e a d e r m a r m e m r t e m d a
t d a r m a t e d a r t d r a t r m r e a r d r e m (11)

(i) d t s i e r i d s i a t a r d i m s i s t r i m e s t a i
d i d m a t i s r a i e i r s t m s i t r d i t i e m t r (14)

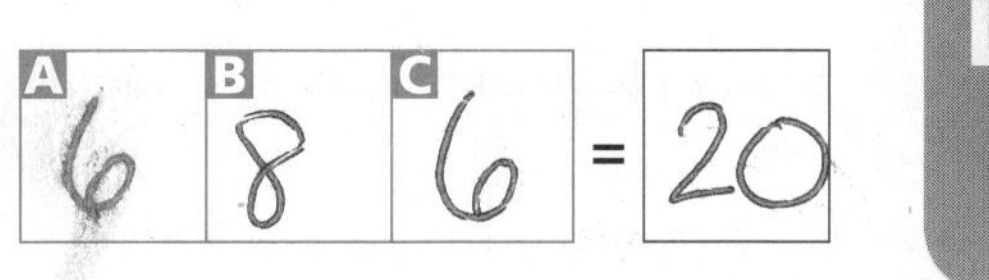

1

m r e i d a s t

2

1. ad
2. at
3. sat
4. sad
5. mad
6. rat
7. eem
8. reem
9. am
10. ram
11. sam

3

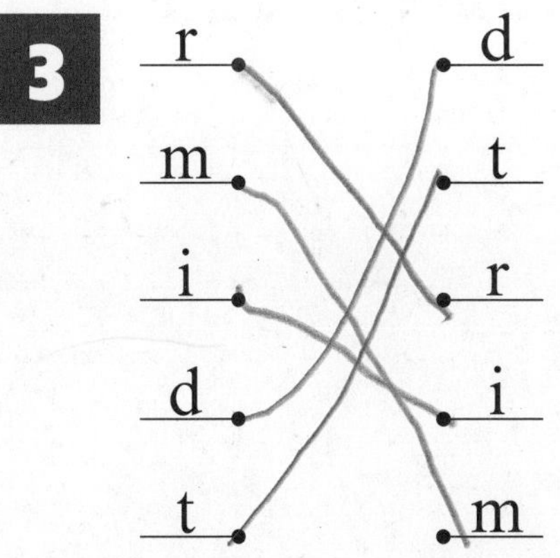

Lesson 5

4

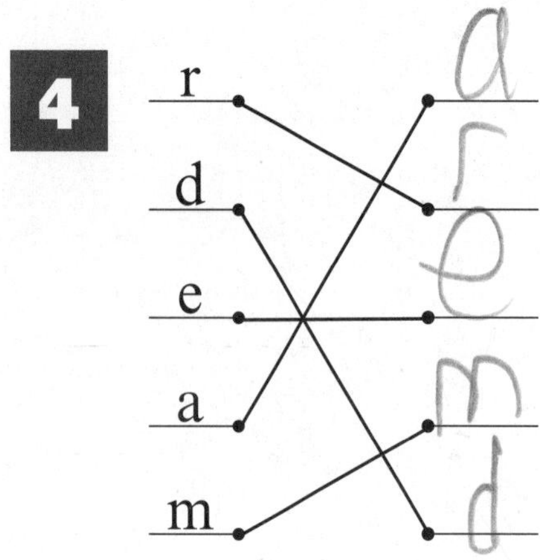

5

(a) d r t a s i e t a d r a m s t d e r a s r e t a s m r t
a r e a r t a s n t d s r a n d a s t n r e a t d a n s (12)

(i) d r i t i r m e i a r i d r i d t i r e a t s m i t e a i
t e i d r i e m e i a s r i d e t m e a d e i t a r s i (14)

(a) s m a r t m e i r i d r a e d e d m a r m a m e a
t d e a d i t d a r s e m e a s t d i e s d a r i a r (10)

A 6 | B 8 | C 6 = 20

Lesson 6

1

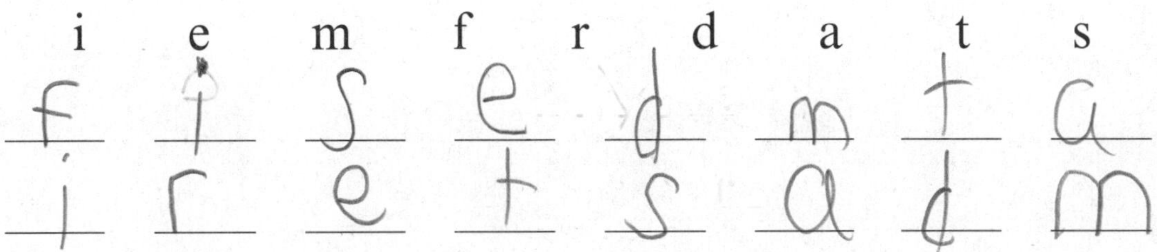

2

1. mat
2. sat

3

1. im
2. if
3. it
4. sa
5. eet
6. reem
7. fit
8. seem
9. ad
10. fa
11. sad

4

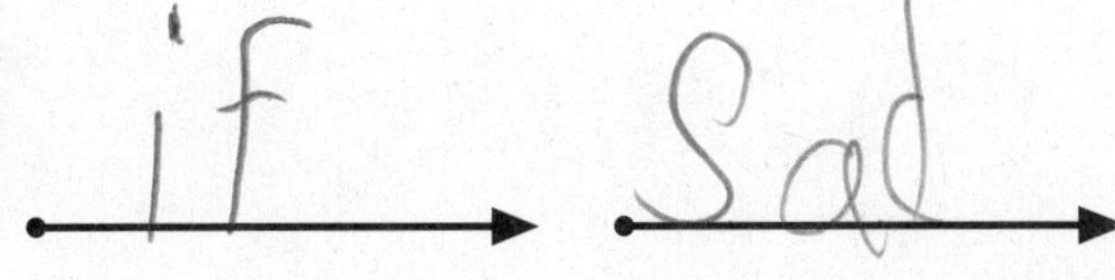

5

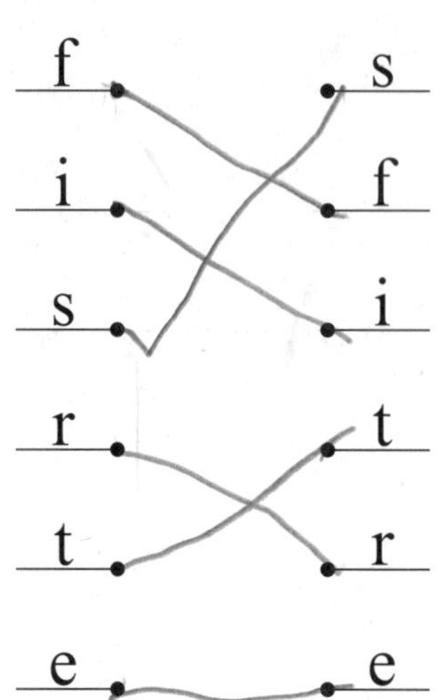

6

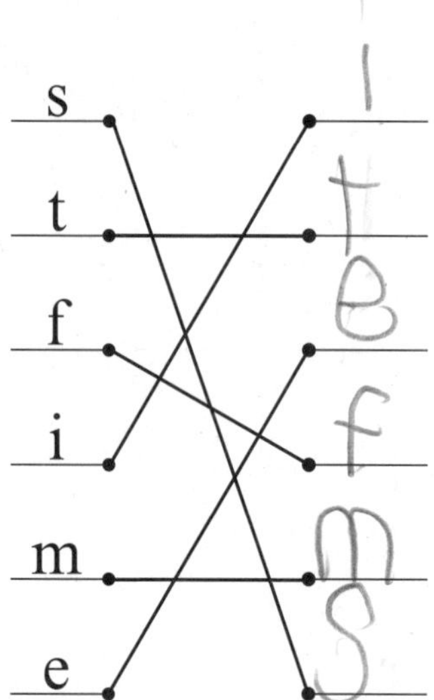

7

(f) m f i r d a t s f m i r d f t f d i f m e m e m f t
f t m f t m f m e m f m e r m e f e r d f e d f e (13)

(t) f t i r d f i t m f i t f d f m t m f e r m i r a t s f t
f t i s f a i s f i t f i t i r m f i r m f s t r s i f r t (11)

(f) t i r e d f i m f i t i f m a s i f i e m f i d s a s m d f
t i e m d i f t i e m d i f m e d i f e t f e d f r t r f f (13)

A 6 B 8 C 6 = 20

Lesson 7

1

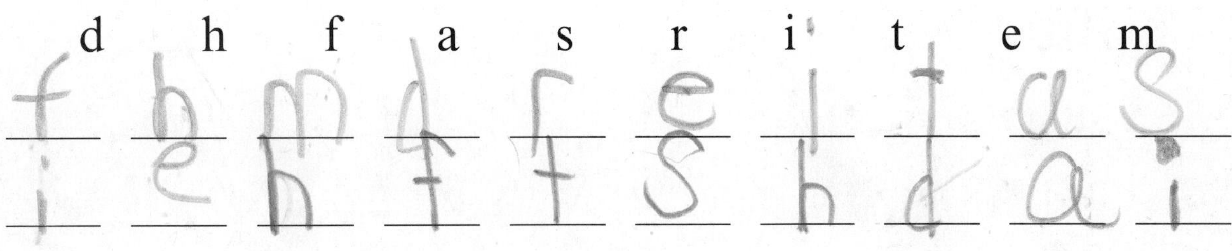

2

1. fat 2. mat 3. rat

3

1. if 2. at 3. mass

4. miss 5. fee 6. feed

7. sit 8. fat 9. rim

10. mitt 11. seem 12. id

4

Lesson 7

5

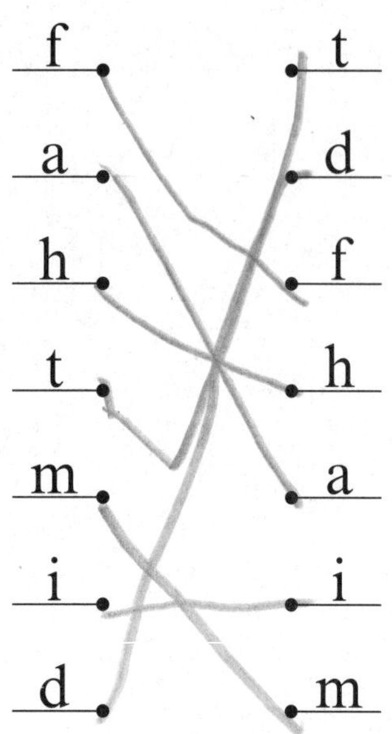

6

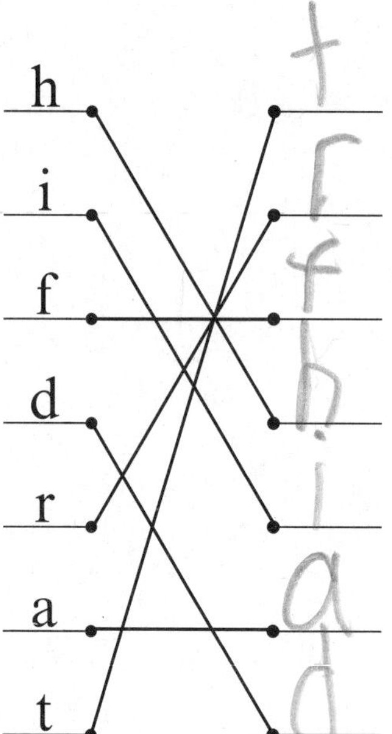

7

(i) d r m i f i d i h r a t e a h e f i t i f m r a e r s r
i t i f m r t r f t d i t t s f i t m e t i m e r i f t i (12)

(h) a d h r t e r i s m d r h s m h i s e f h t f r f h t
e r d f h s a t e h t e r f i f t h s t i s h a m e h i (10)

(t) e t s h s m h t r e h i f h r m r e h t f a d t h e
s d i h t i m e r s t d e f i d t r i m e t s f h e a (8)

A | B | C | =

1

2

1. eed
2. eed

3

1. me
2. see
3. mid
4. seem
5. miss
6. sit
7. rim
8. ram
9. fat
10. mitt

4

1.
2.
3.

5

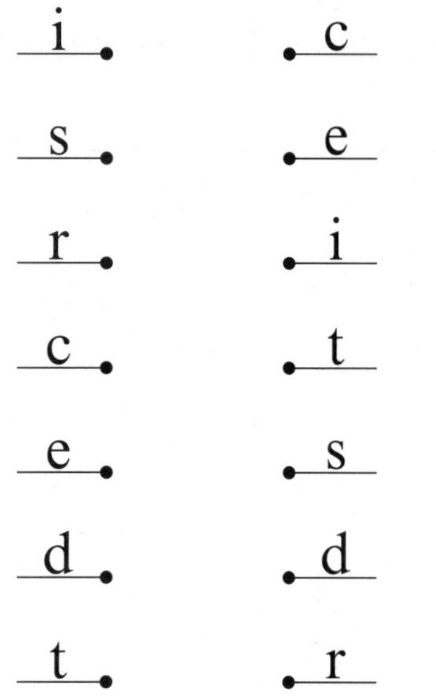

6

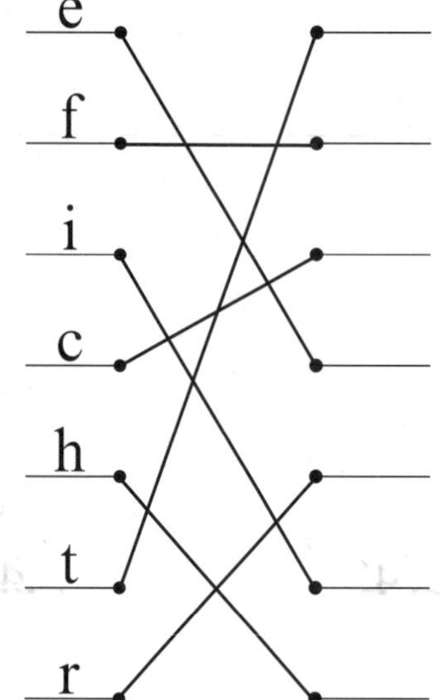

7

(c) s f c e r i t a m c t a r c f d e i c t a m i d c t c
h f c h c s i c d e f d c i d e c r i f t c d e r i m (12)

(d) f d h t i s i e h t h s d h e h t f e i d h e a h s e
f t i d h e t i f d h e i t h f i e d s h e h a s e d (7)

(c) s f c a r e a m e t t h r e d c e t a c d e t i f s h
c a e f t h e h s e c s e h s a c a e f h t c e h c a (8)

A | B | C | =

1

2

1. ad
2. ad

3

1. me
2. see
3. mad
4. rid
5. am
6. ham
7. reed

4

1.
2.
3.

5

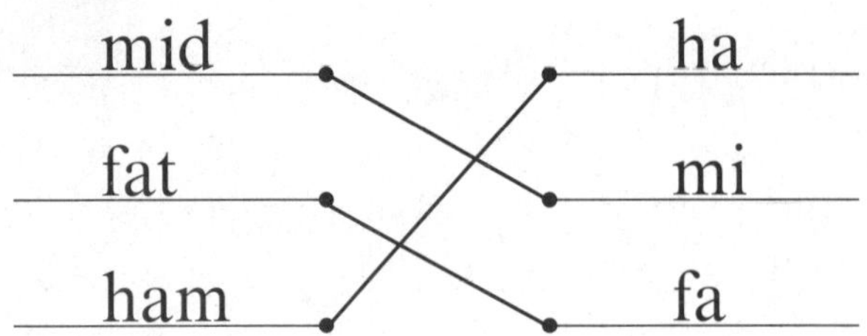

6

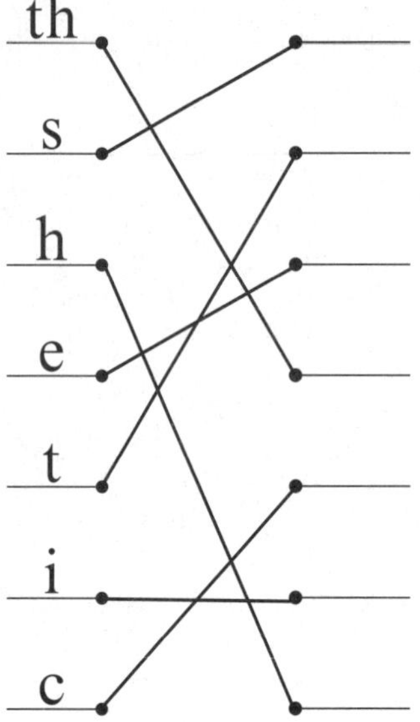

7

(t) t f i e h d t h f h e d h a i s h f t h f h e d h e d
e i f h t i e h f i t h e i f a s h d h e i t h f e i d (6)

(f) f i e d h e i f t h e i d i f e i f e i d h e h d a h e
i e f e h d t i e h f e t f t e h d f i e t f e a s h f (10)

(h) e h d i f h e i s i f h e i d i f h t e i d h e t s a h
e t f h e f h d h a h e d h e t f i e h d i t h e d i (13)

A B C =

1

____ ____ ____ ____ ____ ____ ____ ____ ____

____ ____ ____ ____ ____ ____ ____ ____ ____

2

1. eet
2. eet

3

1. reef
2. this
3. that
4. at
5. mat
6. mad
7. mast
8. if
9. hit
10. feed

4

1. →
2. →
3. →

5

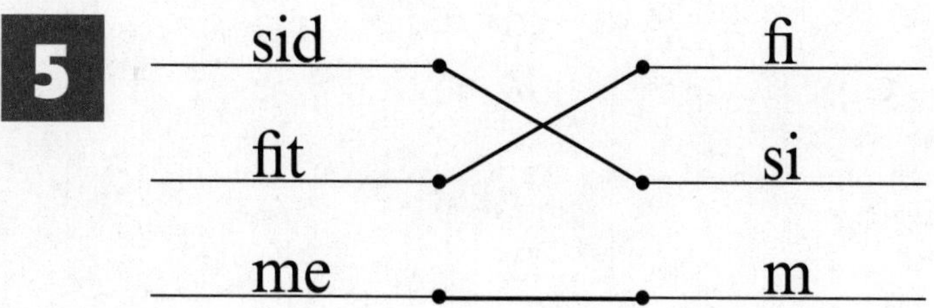

6

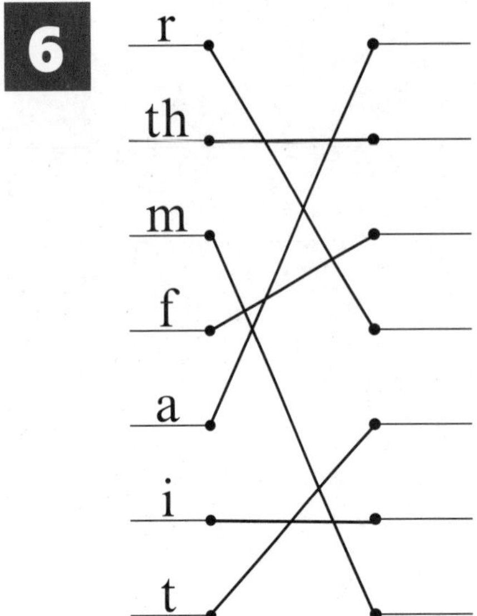

7

(th) r i t h s i f h e s a t h e f h t s t h f h e h e h t h e s h t h f e h t f h t h f e t e f h t f h e t h f e s (7)

(h) r t h a m e n a t m e a d e f e n h e m a s i e n h e m t h a n s m e n f h t e n a s m t n f h e n (6)

(t) r i t h a m e n f h e d t h d i e d a n f m e n t f e n d m e t n f h e n d e t d a e t e h f m e t (7)

A | B | C | =

1

____ ____ ____ ____ ____ ____ ____

____ ____ ____ ____ ____ ____ ____

2

1. it
2. it

3

1. feed
2. reef
3. had
4. hid
5. hat
6. that
7. this
8. the
9. cam
10. cat

4

1.
2.
3.

5

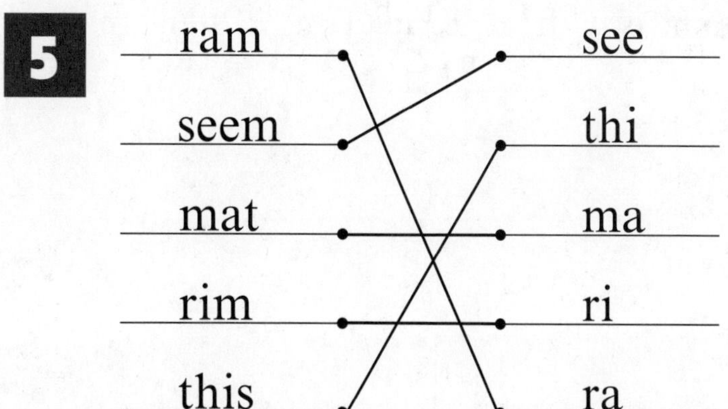

6

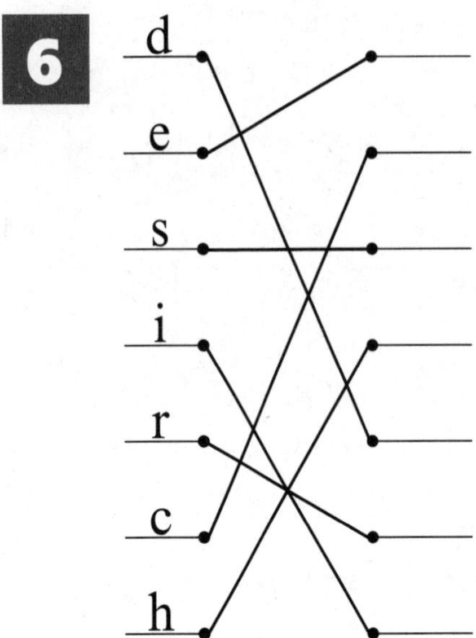

7

(th) r i m t h s c i e l t h s i e h f e h s h e t f e h t h
e t d h t h f e h t e i d l s d i f t h e f h e i t h f (6)

(th) m t h i s h t h t h e l s s i f h t h e i f h t e i f h e
t h e i f h e h t l f m e n t h e f n e a h t h t n e (7)

(th) n e t h e f e t n t h m f h t e n f m t h e f n e t
f h t e t h s h e t h n e m t n e t h m e t h e m e (7)

A B C =

1

______ ______ ______ ______ ______ ______ ______

______ ______ ______ ______ ______ ______ ______

2

1. am → 2. am →

3

1. ham → 2. cat → 3. hat → 4. the →
5. rim → 6. that → 7. fees → 8. rid →
9. mast →

4

1. → 2. → 3. →

5

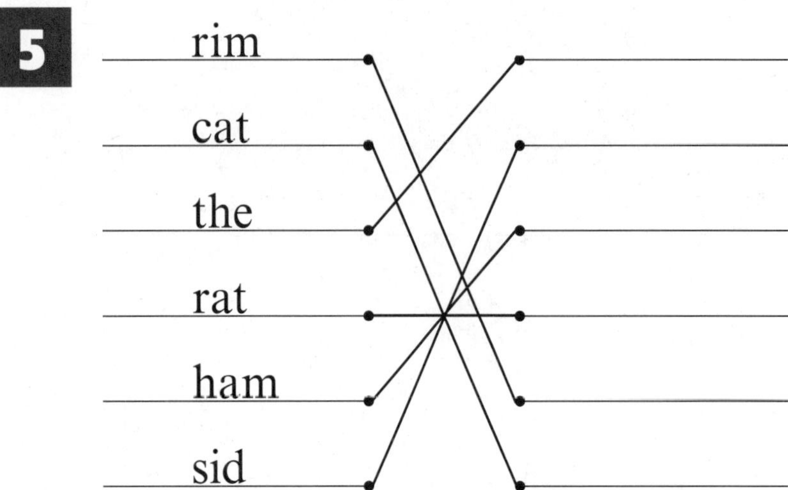

6

(h) m e n t h m e n t h e n f d h e n f m e n t h e n
s m e n d h e m n f t m e n d h s n e m d n t h (7)

(th) m e t h d n e f m t f i t h s h i h t h f i e f h t h
e f t e h f n e m t h e n f m e d n f i e h t h d i (6)

(t) t h e l d m i a n d i e h f t n e d e f e e d m e n t
f d n e t m e t h d i e f t d f e d f i t h e d l f i t (8)

A B C =

1

2

1. at 2. at 3. at

3

1. she 2. dad 3. rid 4. did

5. sad 6. hams 7. seem 8. rims

9. sham

4

1. 2. 3.

5

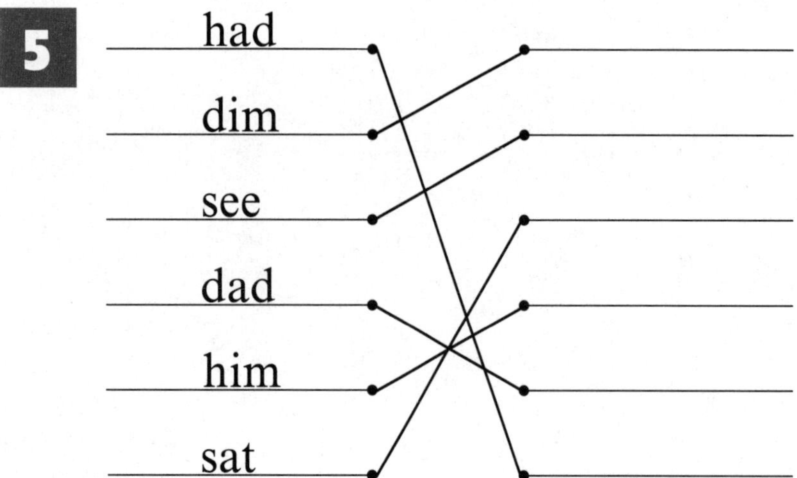

6

(sh) a r s t h s h t h e h s h e h t h f d s d h e s h e t
h e s h t f e s d e f s h t h f h e s d s f h s t s h (6)

(th) a r t h s i e s h i f t h f i e d h f e d t h f e h d h
s f t h e d f e f d t h s f h t d t h f h e h f h t e (6)

(sh) s i e h f s h e m t h e s h f t h e f n e s d e f s h
f h t e n f s h s f s f e n d s h e f m e t s h f e n (6)

1

2

1. it
2. it

3

1. he
2. this
3. hats
4. did
5. rams
6. that
7. him
8. the
9. reefs
10. she

4

1.
2.
3.

5

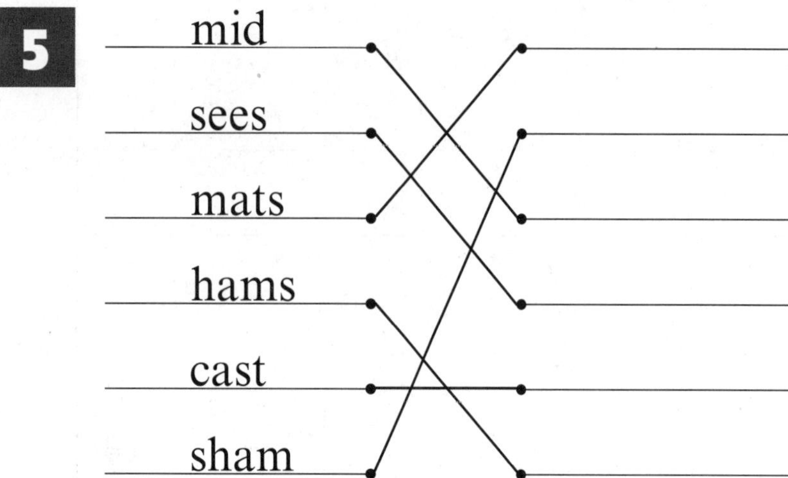

6

(sh) t h s h f h e s h f e s f e d d s d s h t h f e s s l
h e h s d h d e h s h f e h d h s h e h f h e h s h (6)

(th) r i t h s l s m e n s h t e n f m s t h e f e m s e n
t h f e m s n e f t h e n f d e d t h f e n d f h t (5)

(sh) l s f e h s h f e s h f e t h f h s h d e n f h e l d
m e s n e m d h s n e h s f n e s h e m s n e f s h (5)

A B C =

Lesson 15

1

2

1. id
2. id

3

1. tim
2. rats
3. cad
4. dim
5. he
6. shim
7. cast
8. fist
9. she
10. reefs
11. that
12. cats
13. sheet

4

1.
2.
3.

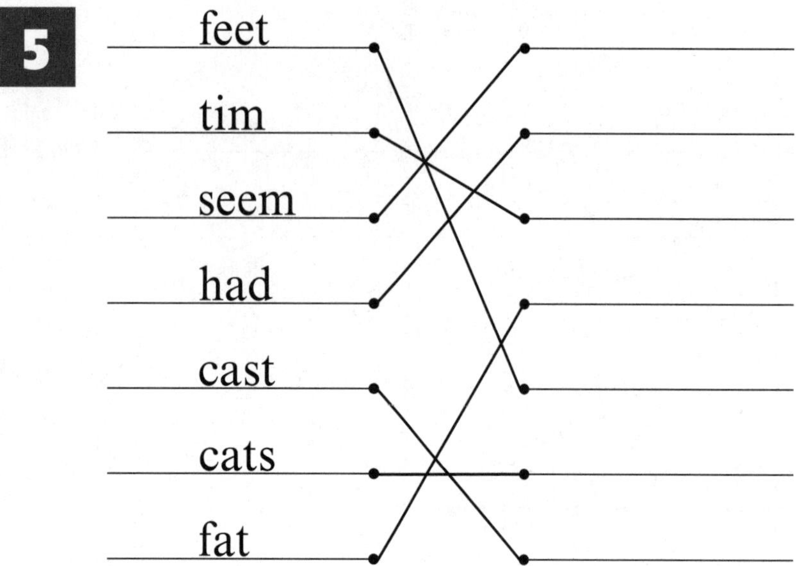

6

(n) m n r e n r m e a r t n s m t h s n e m n t f t m
a t n e m s n t a h s e r t m e n r m e n t r m s (9)

(sh) t h i s h e i f h s h e h f d t h s d t h s t s h t e i
h s h e f s d f s h e t s h t f d s d t s h m f e s n (7)

(th) s h e e t h f i s h e f t h i d r i m r i t h r t d t e
n e t h f m e n t h s e h e f h s d t h t f e d f h d (6)

A | B | C | = |

1

2

1. eem
2. eem

3

1. fist
2. fit
3. fits
4. cats
5. me
6. can
7. cast
8. fast
9. dim
10. din
11. an
12. tan
13. sheets

4

1.
2.
3.

5

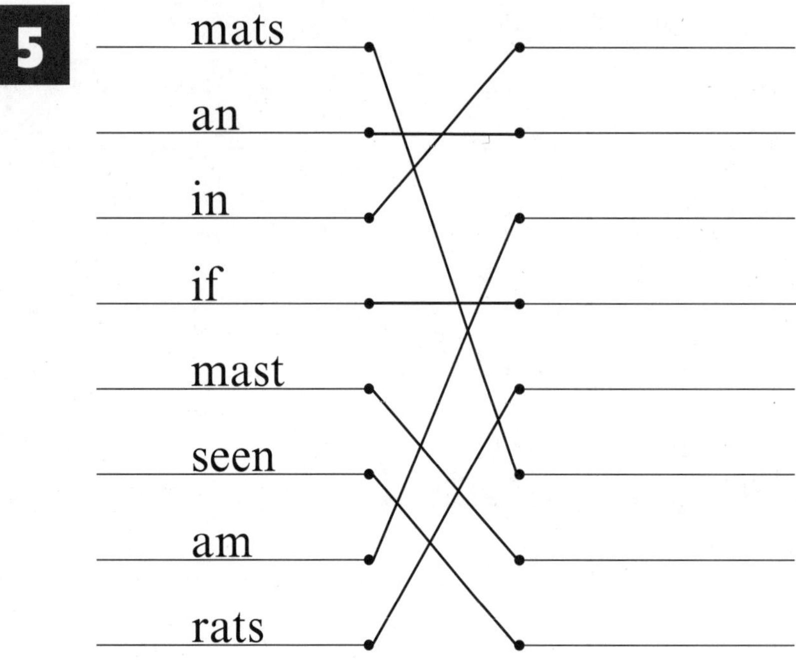

6

(th) f t i t h s f h t e t h f s e d i f h t e f t h f s e d e
t h f e d f s a e t h e d f f s h t e f t h e f d e t h (7)

(n) m n e r m e n r n e m s a n e m s r e n c n e r
n e n d m h e n m d n e h d n e m e n t r n e (13)

(sh) t h i s h f i s h f h e h d t h e d s h e d h s h e
f s h t h s f h t e s h f e h s e s d t f s h t e d a (7)

A | B | C | =

1

______ ______ ______ ______ ______ ______ ______

______ ______ ______ ______ ______ ______ ______

2

1. ad → 2. ad →

3

1. sat → 2. fish → 3. ram → 4. ran →
5. dim → 6. din → 7. feet → 8. feed →
9. he → 10. him → 11. she → 12. had →
13. fast → 14. cats →

4

1. → 2. → 3. →

5

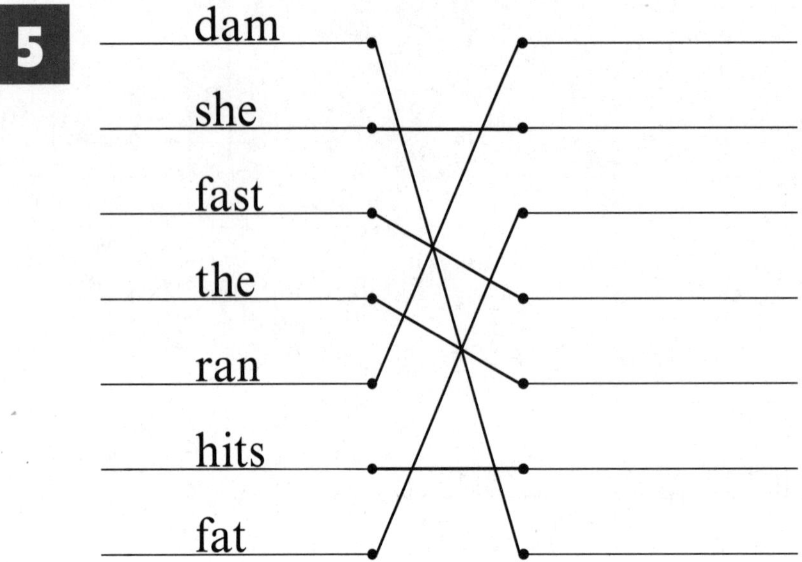

6

(sh) t h f s h i f d t h s t i f s h t e d s h s t h e d f s d
t s h t e i s h t i f d i s h e d f s h t s f t i s h e d (8)

(n) m e n t h s n t h e s e n t m e n t h s n e r e n
m r n e m r n t e m s n e a n s n e m r i m e n (12)

(th) m e t h d i s h t h e f i s h d i d t h e s h e t d f
t f t h f h t i s m e r e t h r d t r h t d t h e h t h (7)

1

2

1. in
2. in

3

1. is
2. can
3. dim
4. ash
5. mad
6. feet
7. she
8. he
9. had
10. ram
11. seem
12. him
13. did
14. need

4

1.
2.
3.

5

She had rats and cats.

6

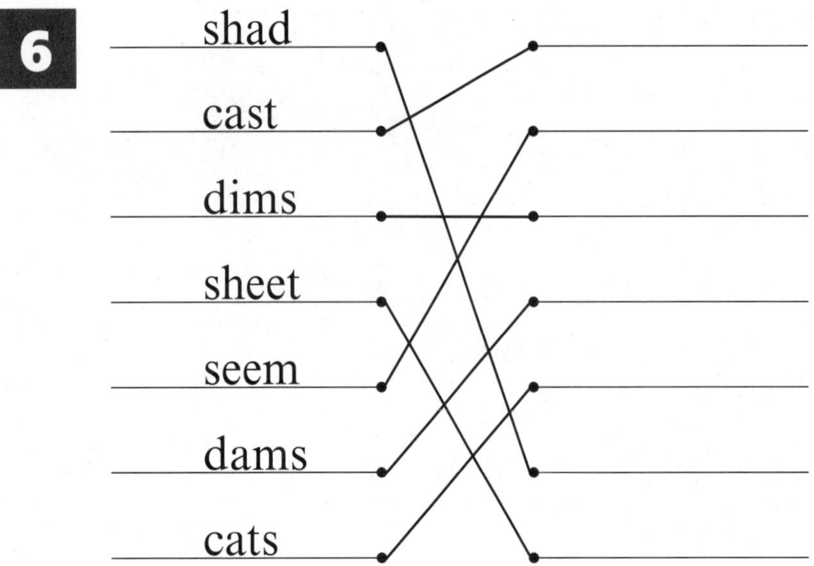

7

(h) f d h t h e f i s h d e h d h e t f e s h d e h t h d
h e t h d i e h d i s h e i t i f s e r h e m s n e n (13)

(sh) t h i s h f i d s h a d f h s t i s f t s n t h s h e i
i f s h e h t i f i s h e t s n m h s h e t n e s h m (7)

(th) f i s t h d i f h t i m t h s i f h e i t h s h e n m
d f h e h t d t h e d m e n t h s e i f h t h s t h (7)

A	B	C	=	
			=	

1

2

1. eed 2. eed

3

1. am 2. if 3. an 4. it
5. ash 6. the 7. has 8. fast
9. she 10. in 11. cats 12. fins
13. hits 14. he 15. is 16. that

4

1. 2. 3.

5

A fish has fins.

Lesson 19

6

7

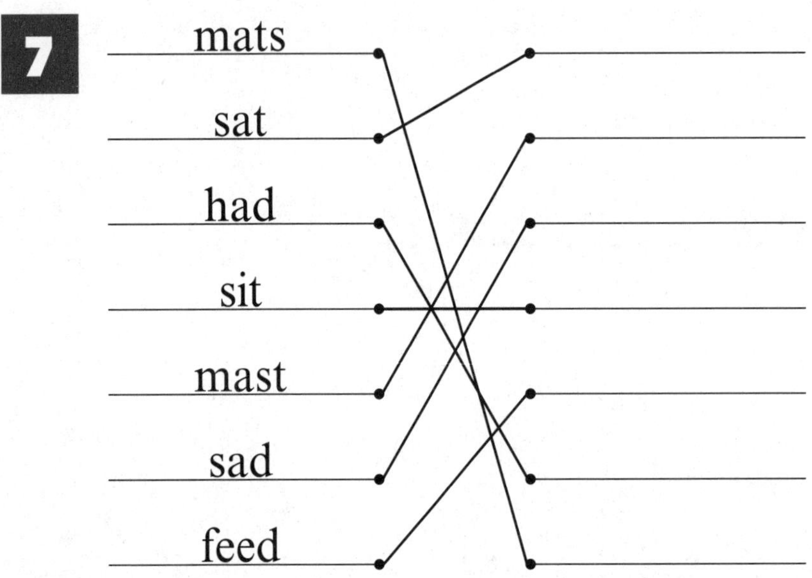

8

(o) c o a e s o a s t h a o s e h t m e n o a h e n o
e h s n i o c e c o i c o a s o e i s o e t h s n e (10)

(th) m i t h r i d s h e e t h r h t f t h i f h e i d h t h
i f e t d i r f r t h d i t h d t d r f t h f d t f t h (8)

(sh) s h o r e d i s h t h i n f a s h t d e o s i f h t s h
h e d h s t e s h f h t h e s h f h t h e h i f s h t e (7)

A B C =

Lesson 20

1

2

1. an
2. an

3

the and this ant

hand deed fish did

fast she fins cats

cans has that

4

1.
2.
3.

5

That ram can feed a fish.

Lesson 20

6

7

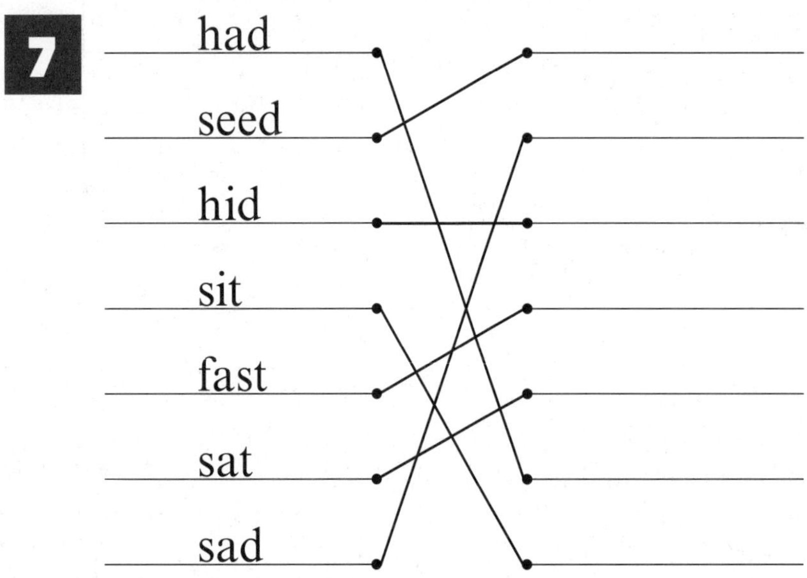

8

(sh) s h a d t h s d t h e s h e d o e s h e d t s f t s h
f e t f s h e f h s t s h t e d s d e s h t s n e s h (8)

(o) c o a e c i t h s o i e i s o e i s c a s i e o s i a o
e i a i s e o s i a i s o i e o a s c o e i c e o c e (10)

(th) t h s d i t h e s h t s h t h i s h t f s h t f t h s e h
f h t e t h f i s t h e i f t d t h e d f t h e s o e h s (8)

1

2

1. 2.

3

need this fast fist

hand seems rims had

dish dash and cash

that hats did

4

1. 2. 3.

5

His cats ran fast.

6

1. see 2. tha 3. fi 4. fi

7

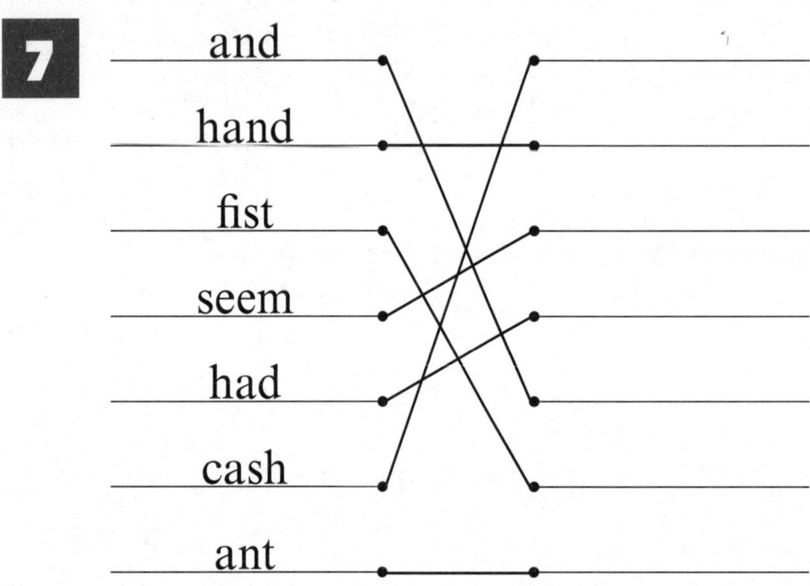

8

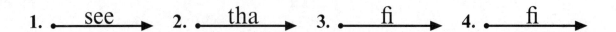

(i) l i t h s i s h f t h s i d f e i d h f t h e i f i d l i d h e f h d i e f h e a d i h s l d i e h f i s h d i e (12)

(o) o s o a o s c o a o s d i a o s t o a s o t l a s i o e d a o s n e m s i a c i e a o c i s a n c o c i s n a (12)

(sh) s h a i f l s h a i f h s l a h s i f h s h a f h s l a d s h e i d s a h a s l e i s h a i f d e d i t s h a f l i s (6)

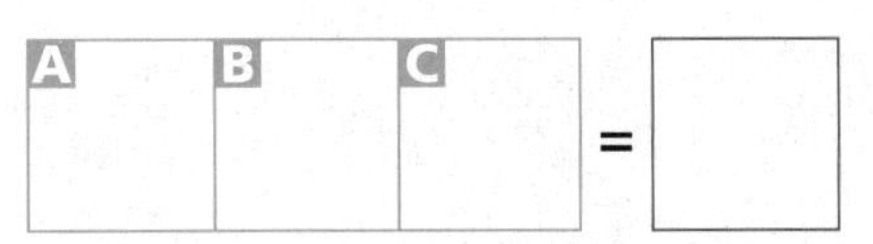

1

_____ _____ _____ _____ _____ _____

_____ _____ _____ _____ _____ _____

2

1. __________ 2. __________

3

him math teeth did

dash cash dish she

cast not nod the

con can and

4

1. __________ 2. __________ 3. __________

5

That ram sat on an ant.

6

1. si 2. fi 3. cat

4. nee 5. ha

7

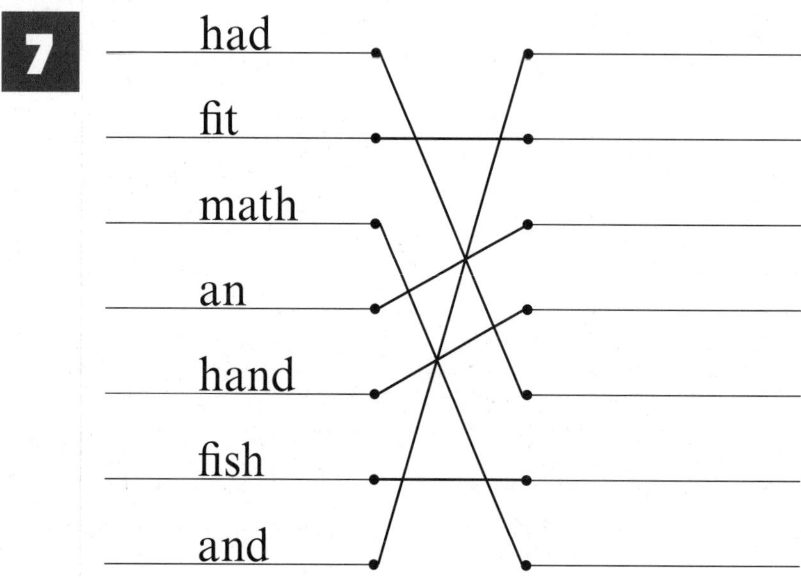

8

(th) t h s i d l s i d h e d t f h d e t h f h d h e s i d
i f t h d e l f i d e t h d i e f i d h e f t h e i d l (5)

(g) t h g i s l i f h s e i d c a l d i h e m g h d s m
t g h c d m e h t s g h c m a s h e g c g h s i (6)

(sh) t h s i f h s i d s h e i f l s i d h s h e h d i f s d
d s h f e i d f s h e i f a s l s h d i e s g d s h e i (6)

A B C =

1

2

1. ______ 2. ______ 3. ______

3

rims seen rams feet

cast hand tan cash hands

dish tin had sheets

teen if on shot

4

1. ______ 2. ______ 3. ______

Lesson 23

5

1. She has cats.
2. He needs a tin dish.
3. It is in the hand.

6

1. hee 2. tha 3. di 4. tha

7

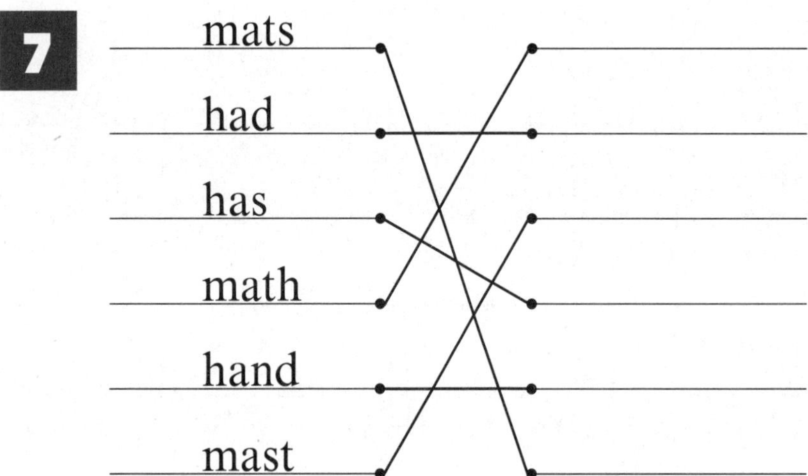

8

(c) o c a o s o e o c o s o e t h a o s n e m a c n s e
m c n e s o a o e s c n e o s c o s e a n s o c o s (7)

(o) o a n d e m a d n c m e a n d o c o a m e d c o
d c o a h e s o c o e a h t o s c a o s c h e o s (10)

(th) t h s i e m s i e h t s t h d i s s h e t h e i d l d f
t e h t h e i d t h d a h d t h d l e a n d m t h e d (7)

A B C =

1

2

1. ____ 2. ____ 3. ____

3

mass math than this that

the teeth seems mist dad

feed did sheets reefs deed

4

1. ____ 2. ____ 3. ____

5

1. A shad can not sing.
2. Dad did math.
3. She can see that reef.

Lesson 24

6

1. shee 2. mis 3. fas 4. ha

7

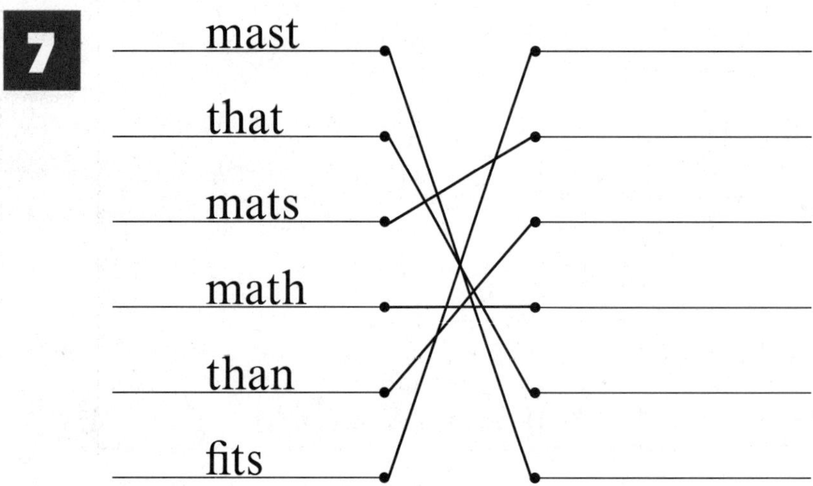

8

(f) f i g t h e d f h e d h f h d h e h s h f e i d l e i f h e i f l a s o r h s o r i f h s h e h f i e s h a l s (8)

(th) t h d i h t d i t h f h t e f h d e f t h e i d l f i e h s d h t h f h e i f i l s i d h t h f e h s i f l e t d (5)

(g) g i g f i d s d g i d h e i f a r a g h s i c h e g h a s h g c h a i e c h g l a o g h s i e o c h g i e s g s (10)

1

_____ _____ _____ _____ _____ _____

_____ _____ _____ _____ _____ _____

2

1. __________ **2.** __________ **3.** __________

3

cats sheets cast math

mats dam sees feet

feed dim din clan

4

1. __________ **2.** __________ **3.** __________

5

1. She had a shad.
2. That dash is fast.
3. He has rats and cats.

Lesson 25

6

1. da 2. tha 3. di 4. tha

7

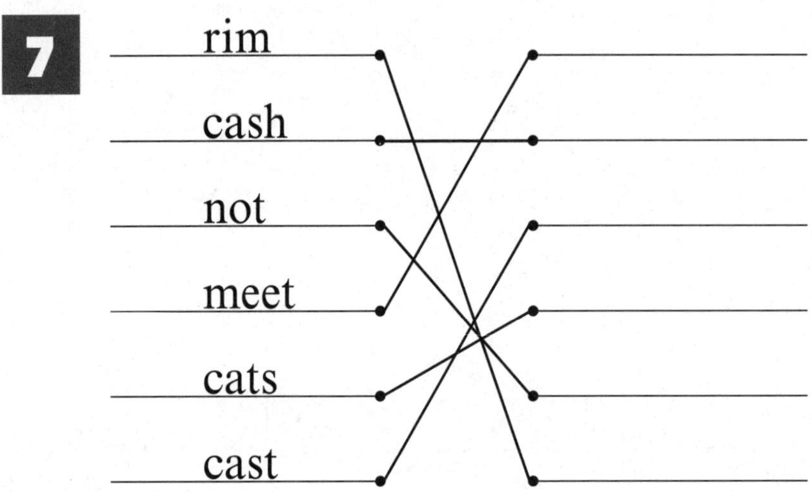

8

(sh) s h t i h s i f h g i e h s l f i s h f i s d e t h s i s h
h s t f i l s h f e i f l s i f h e i s h f i h s i f l s h (6)

(g) g a r o a i c o a i c o t h a l c g h s m e s h a m
n a g h a m a h g m e i a c h g m o c h g o a c (6)

(o) o a r i o a i r o c i e o c o e i t h a o d l t h e i
a n d i o e o a i d n e l t o a d h t i a o e c i e o (11)

A | B | C = ___

1

1. ________ 2. ________ 3. ________ 4. ________

2

1. ________ 2. ________ 3. ________

3

___ ___ ___ ___ ___ ___

___ ___ ___ ___ ___ ___

4

sheets fits cats hams fast

dam din sees mats feed

dan feet dim shad fees

5

1. She did not see him.
2. That fish has a fin.
3. A cat had sand on his feet.
4. She hid in the hen shed.

6

1. thi 2. rat 3. hi 4. sho

7

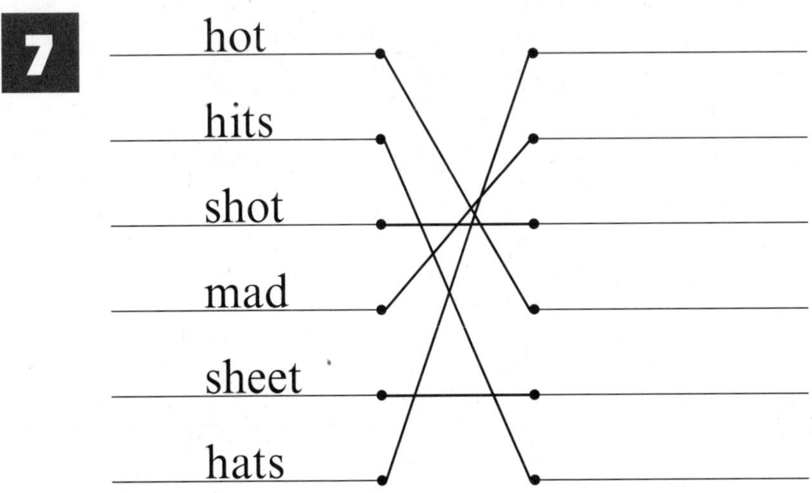

8

(n) m n o i s n f o e i f o n f m e n t l f i t h n m n
t r m r n r m e n r a r i e f m r n f m s n r m s (10)

(g) g o i a o s o i f h t o i f h a g o a h e i r a h r o
f n e o r m f h e o f g m r o r h e m r n a f g m (4)

(d) d o r h e o t h e t l a h d f o e h f h t n e m d
e n t m d n e h t m a d h t h e n d l f m t n e h (6)

A B C = ____

1

1. ________ 2. ________ 3. ________

4. ________ 5. ________

2

1. ________ 2. ________ 3. ________

3

____ ____ ____ ____ ____ ____

____ ____ ____ ____ ____ ____

4

not mod hot odd

if in an and

on it mist than

that teeth rims sand

5

1. Can she see if it is dim?
2. She met him and me.
3. He met them on the ant hill.

6

1. fi . tha

7

seems

math

fits

hand

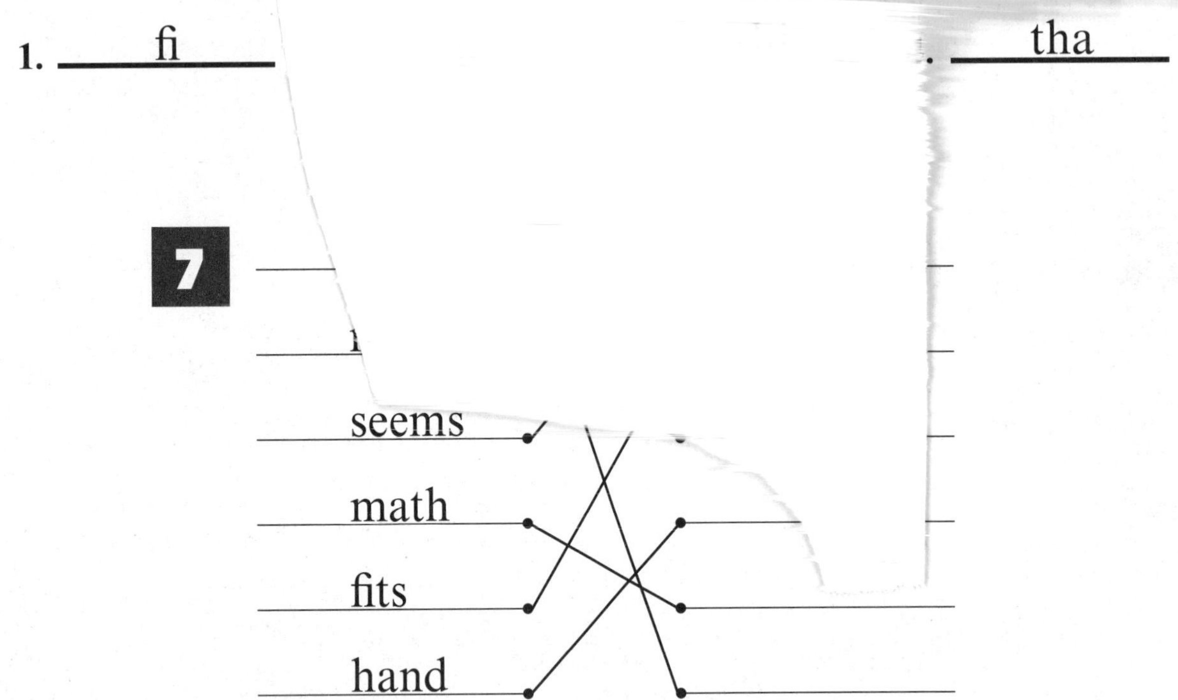

8

(th) g o i t h e i h t o i t h l f m e n t h s h t e f h t h
s h e h f i e l d s h t h f h e i d s f h t i e t f h i (5)

(t) t i f l e i d l o s i f h e i f l t i e o f h t e i d s o d
f i e h f t h e i f l t o e f i t h e i f o t e l f t h t o (9)

(d) d h e h t i d l a h d h e l t h d i r l d h e h d i
l d a l f i e h s o d i e h f a l d i s h e h f i e d (10)

A | B | C | = |

Lesson 28

1

1. ______ 2. ______ 3. ______

4. ______ 5. ______

2

1. ______ 2. ______ 3. ______

3

____ ____ ____ ____ ____ ____

____ ____ ____ ____ ____ ____

4

teen hand kiss keen kin

sand meek seek sick mint

got gash dim rim deed

5

1. He had cash in his hand.
2. Did she see the deed?
3. Ten wet rats sat in the mash.

Lesson 28

6

1. ______th______ 2. ______th______ 3. ______th______ 4. ______th______

7

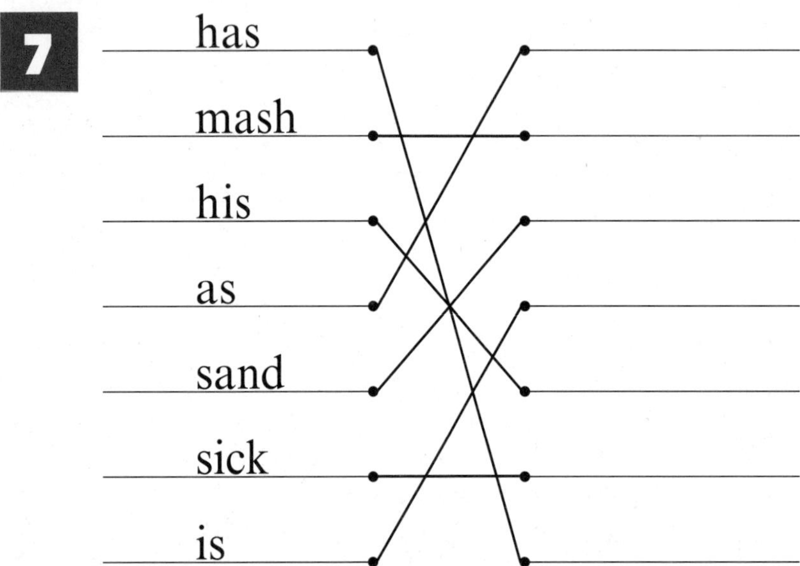

8

(k) h t i s k f i l s a l f i s k s h e i f l k a l s k f n k
a l r i e h a n f i k e n a l s k f i e h t n f k t h k (9)

(g) g o a i s o c i a o o g i c i a o e m c a i e i t h a i o
g o a s i o f h e g a o e i d h g l e m a s n e g h o c (6)

(sh) t h i a l s i h s h e i a l s h e i d l s h a l d i e h
l s h d l i e h t s h a l s l k e h s h e i a s k e h s (6)

A B C =

1

1. ______ 2. ______ 3. ______

4. ______ 5. ______ 6. ______

2

1. ______ 2. ______ 3. ______

3

___ ___ ___ ___ ___ ___

___ ___ ___ ___ ___ ___

4

did dad deed mint sheets

fins kiss kit ash odd sod

sin sash seems math mash

5

1. Can she sit on ten tan mats?

2. An ant is not fast in the dash.

3. She got sand and ants in the dish.

6

1. fi 2. th 3. ra 4. ha

7

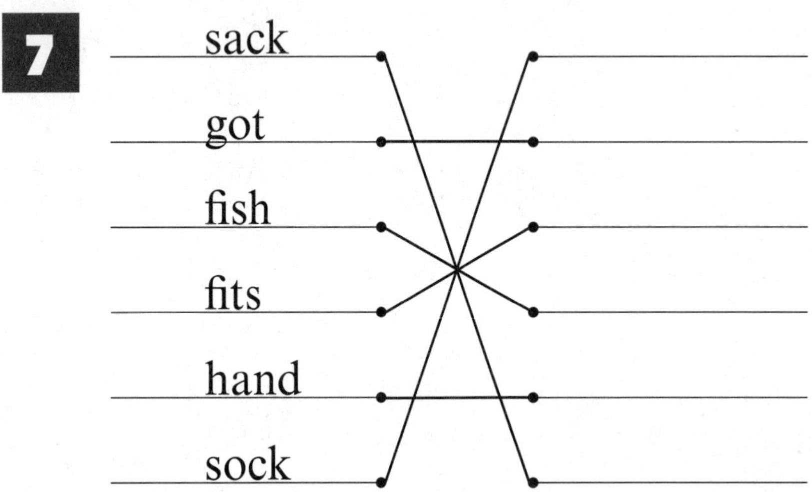

8

(ck) c k t h s l c k s i d h c h t i d l c h c k t h s i k c
h i d c k c d l a k d s e k c k a l s h d c d t h c k (6)

(n) m a n o n s o m e n a o s l e m a n s f l e h m a l
m f r n t l e m a s l m f e n s l a i s o f n e t m l (7)

(sh) s h t i s h s l s h c l s h d i d c h a l i d h s l s h
d i t h c t s h c l a i s d e i s l c h s h c l a h s d (7)

A | B | C =

1

1. ________ 2. ________ 3. ________

4. ________ 5. ________ 6. ________

2

1. ________ 2. ________ 3. ________

3

____ ____ ____ ____ ____ ____

____ ____ ____ ____ ____ ____

4

rim trim shad tree rod

trod cad cod kid kick

sick sack than this rags

5

1. Did he get mad at his cats?

2. Can she kick that sack?

6

1. th________ 2. da________ 3. th________

4. sh________ 5. see________

Lesson 30

7

She had 3 fish.

This fish is a shad.

This fish is a cod.

This fish is in the cat.

8

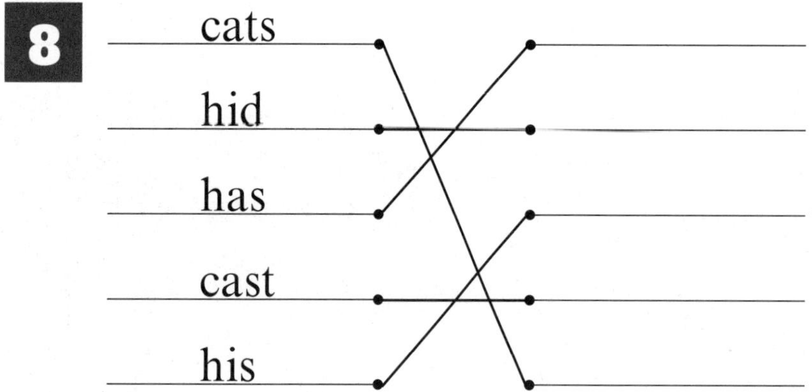

9

(d) t h d i e l s o d i c l a h s i c h e i d l s i s o l e d
c i d l s i c h g h s i s d l e i d h g h s i o d s l e (8)

(ck) c k t h d i f h g c a l s k d i c f l d c k d i f h o a
d c d t c k d i s l c k d i a l s i c k a l s c k e i t (6)

(g) o a k g l s h r h d n m g n s m e n g l a s h g n
l t h s e n t l g m s o a l s e m g n a h l s e i l t (6)

A | B | C | = |

1

1. ______ 2. ______ 3. ______

4. ______ 5. ______ 6. ______

2

1. ______ 2. ______ 3. ______

3

____ ____ ____ ____ ____ ____

____ ____ ____ ____ ____ ____

4

rim tree tag trim rocks

kicks met send get mend

kid sacks men tin ten deed

5

1. He did his math as he sat on the mat.

2. Did she get a cast on the leg?

6

1. fi______ 2. see______ 3. ca______

4. shee______ 5. da______

7

He did math.

He did this. (1 + 3 = 5)

Then he did this. (7 + 2 = 4)

Can he add?

8

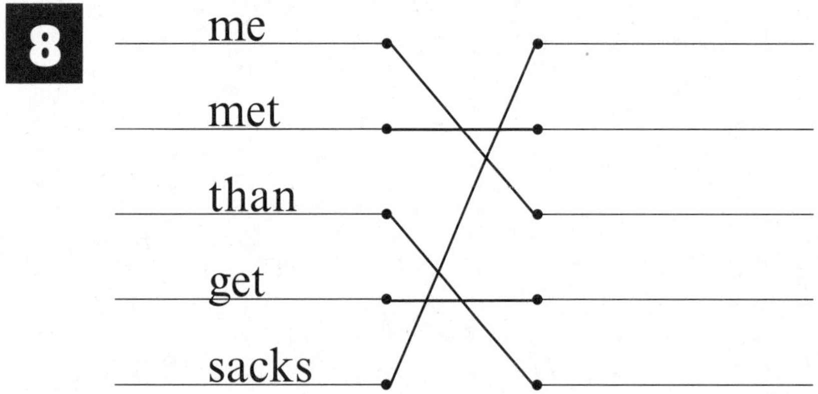

9

(ck) c k s h t l e h s l c d l s l s c k d a l s c k a l k c k
s h e l a h s i t l s o f c k s l s c f l s c k t h e i a (6)

(sh) s h t l e h s f l s i e h s f s h e l s i f h s l c l a m
c s h c l a m s l c o e h s h c a i e l s h l a i d l (5)

(th) t h a l s i e h a m s n t h e a l i s e h t s l a t h
s l a i s h e m d c h t h d i a l d h t i d l a t h d (5)

A | B | C | = |

Lesson 32

1

_____ _____ _____ _____ _____ _____

_____ _____ _____ _____ _____ _____

2

1. __________ 2. __________ 3. __________

4. __________ 5. __________ 6. __________

3

dad did we men mend

seen sent with met meet

socks when send rack

4

1. Can she sit and fish in the mist?

2. Did sand get in the street?

5

1. eet 2. ca 3. ash

4. fi 5. and 6. ad

6

She can mend.

Can she mend a sheet?

Can she mend a sock?

She can not mend this.

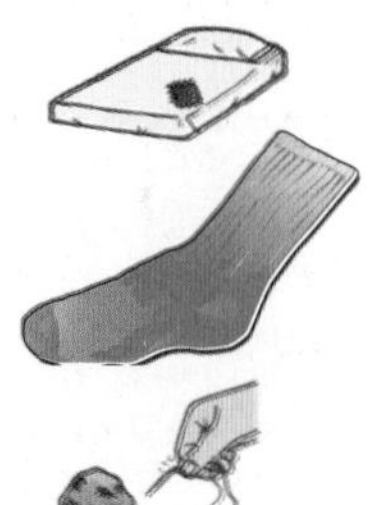

7

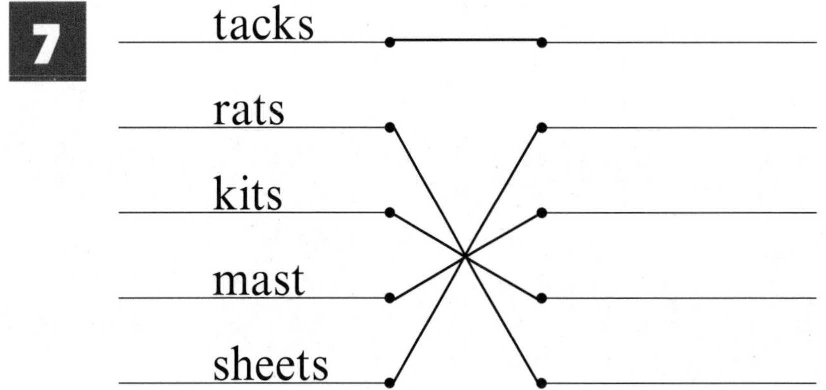

8

(k) k c h t l a s k l c h a l s k e t k l s h f i t l a s k
h f d k a l d s k d h f k l t h e d s d s l k d s k (10)

(g) g h i l a s o c i a s d l r i g h d i r e d o s l d i g
e i s i a s d o e i a s d f l g l a s i e o a h d i g (5)

(sh) s h t h e i s l a i s d f h s d l i a s h d i s l s i d d
s i d s h i e l i s f t h e i l s k t s h f i e s i h s h (5)

A | B | C =

1

2

1. ________ 2. ________ 3. ________

4. ________ 5. ________ 6. ________

3

wish sent man rocks trims

win mend sacks with gash

we wet send men dash

4

1. We did not get wet feet in the street.

2. She did not see him.

3. Can she see when it is dim?

5

1. ___nee___ 2. ___at___ 3. ___ash___

4. ___fi___ 5. ___at___ 6. ___ca___

6

A cat had wet feet.

Then the cat went in wet sand.

That cat went on a street.

The street has wet sand on it.

7

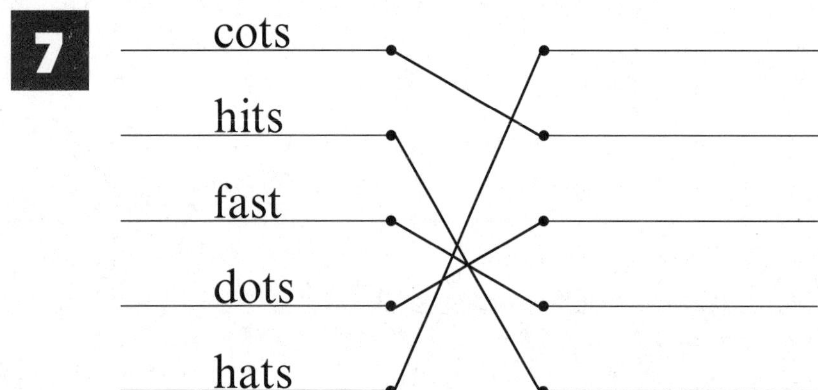

8

(on) tondmfonronacontonelanosonsaflahonfhenoasontheendon (9)

(he) freehethemeslfhsahesalfshelflatandmeheastobehefreetre (6)

(she) sheflthefiatlifesheflsdethishetreeshelfskitheheshemetru (5)

1

______ ______ ______ ______ ______ ______

______ ______ ______ ______ ______ ______

2

1. ____________ 2. ____________ 3. ____________

4. ____________ 5. ____________ 6. ____________

3

his has hams dash dish

mash math kicks sacks did

when with rods trot socks

4

1. She is sad and sick.
2. His fat fish is not fast.
3. She met me at the dam.

5

1. and____ 2. an____ 3. wi____

4. fi____ 5. ma____ 6. eeds____

6

The rams had a meet.

This ram can win when the rams trot.

This ram can win when the rams sing.

When can this ram win?

7

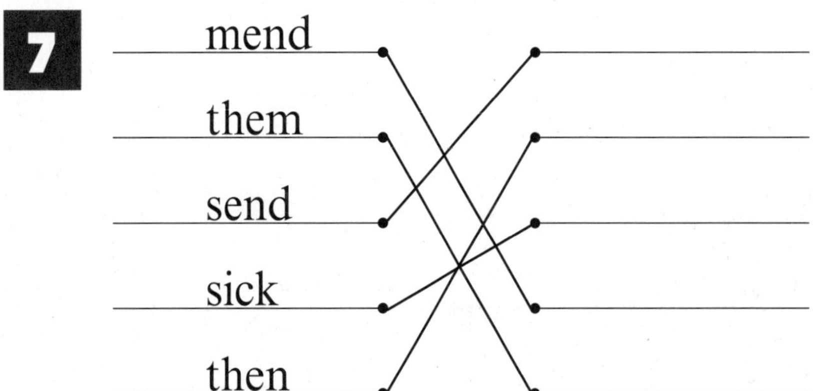

8

(me) tmethesnemenaslemasmenaslnemasremenasmenrlalreremer (6)

(met) setmetmentlretanetandmetfretemetlsmchflaksmetnelkfhet (4)

(if) riftlskfifhtielifheiasflifhtiilelfitheifhtleilfoshifleifltiefo (7)

A | B | C | = |

Lesson 35

1

______ ______ ______ ______ ______ ______

______ ______ ______ ______ ______ ______

2

1. ____________ 2. ____________ 3. ____________

4. ____________ 5. ____________ 6. ____________

3

not nods sheets cash wheel

trees when sand shots trim

dent on if in send

4

1. The ram will not win the dash.

2. When did that man feed his cats?

3. She got wet in the street.

5

1. ca 2. fi 3. em

4. eets 5. fi 6. and

6

He has an ant.

That ant is trim and fast.

It is as fast as a cat.

And it can fit in a hand.

7

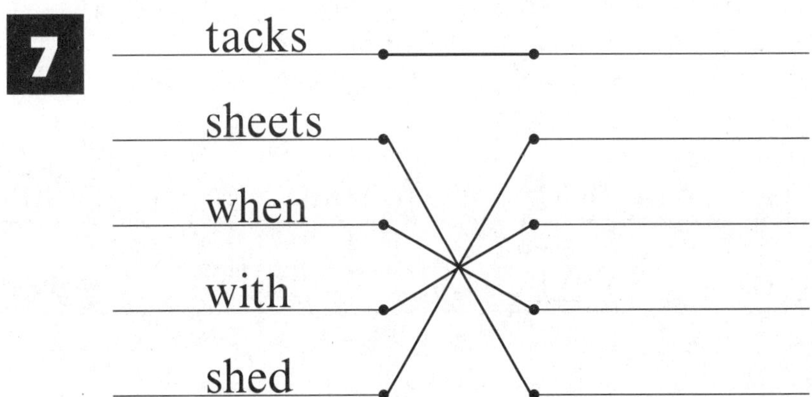

8

(it) itfitlasifilafithfilliasfithfilsfdifhtilealitiflafltifitfhisilt (6)

(we) werfrelisfaliweflaiwemicilaemcaewalsweilafliweliadflwe (6)

(in) tinsilasmwimasdfilniniasdfliasineiflasidiemafilindiaslim (4)

1

____ ____ ____ ____ ____ ____

____ ____ ____ ____ ____ ____

2

1. ________ 2. ________ 3. ________

4. ________ 5. ________ 6. ________

3

got rags than them get

man men rocks gas grim

trim will well

4

1. I wish she had ten cats.
2. When he sings, I get sad.
3. That wheel has wet sand on it.

5

1. en 2. ca 3. shee

4. th 5. th 6. ca

6

A tack sat on the track.

This wheel went on the track.

The tack got in the wheel.

And that wheel did this.

7

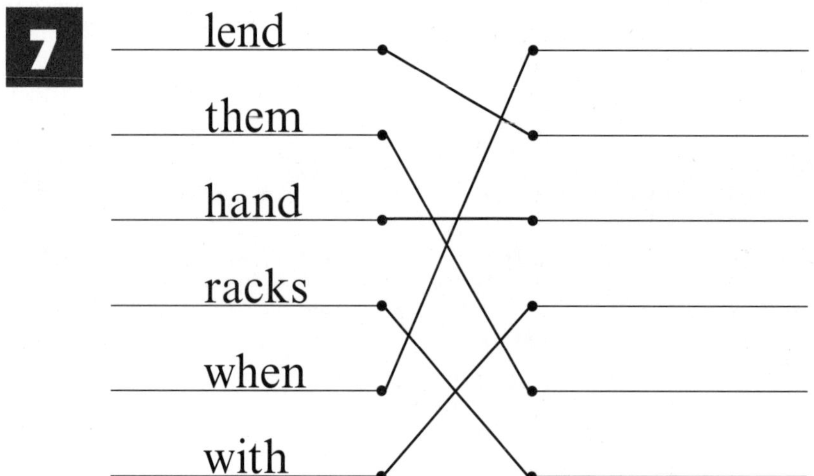

8

(the) thefedelfthedehtetlthealsifhthelsiftdetlitheslatkeslihthe (6)

(if) ifthefiltislifitiwisfliwodifltisliftositliasfitdilaidlfifitla (5)

(on) onmeonoameonaosmeonaoeimtoenaosmieoafnoeaoneomaf (5)

Lesson 37

A | B | C | = |

1

______ ______ ______ ______ ______ ______

______ ______ ______ ______ ______ ______

2

1. ______ 2. ______ 3. ______

4. ______ 5. ______

3

meek mint hand cold sold

shell racks cracks trim tree

trod slam sing sled slid

4

1. Ten cats did not feel well.
2. I did not see that shell.
3. Did she see how fast that ant ran?

5

1. th______ 2. ick______ 3. fa______

4. rim______ 5. ca______ 6. ree______

6

A crack is in the street.

A ram is in the crack.

A rat is on the ram.

This is on the rat.

7

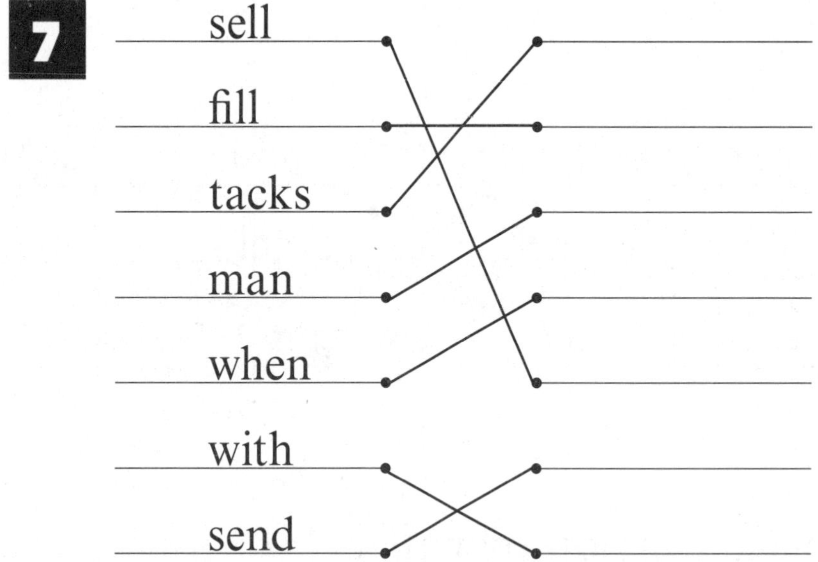

8

(she) shethislandskitheshesdemeheseeshefreesheothesdeknshes (5)

(the) tnesothattheisthefreetheintnefillshethefreethekneetmethe (6)

(is) fissthisthelandsithinisthesitlandthisintinthisniclastoisno (6)

A | B | C =

Lesson 38

1

______ ______ ______ ______ ______ ______

______ ______ ______ ______ ______ ______

2

1. ______ 2. ______ 3. ______

4. ______ 5. ______

3

land win wind her lend letter

sell rent she them hold hill

than slam slid slim told had has

4

1. How hot is it in this shack?
2. If the wheel has a dent, it will not go on the track.
3. She slid her sled on the hill.
4. How well can she sing?

5

1. ___ha___ 2. ___en___ 3. ___la___

4. ___ith___ 5. ___rim___ 6. ___ee___

Lesson
38

6

A seed sat on a rock.

The seed fell in the sand.

The sand got wet.

A tree is in the sand.

7

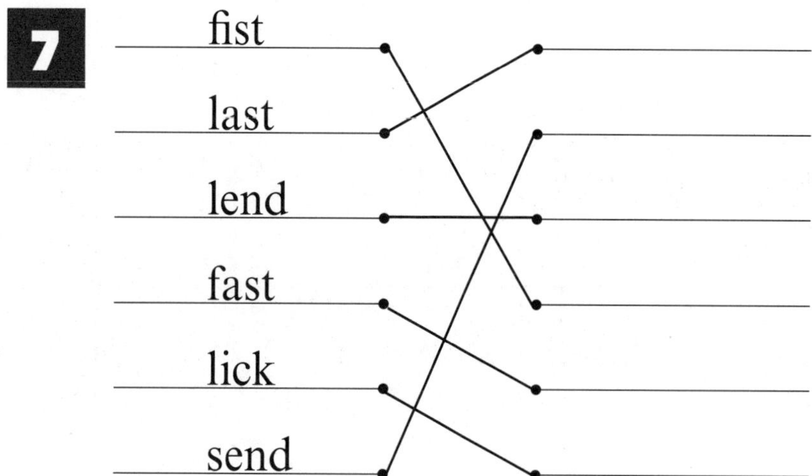

8

(had) r a d m a n n a d h a d s h a d f a d t m a h a t f o r h a d t h e h a d f o r m e t h a d h a s (5)

(has) t h a s t h a t f a s h a s t h e m a s t h a s t r a s l h a s h a c r a s h t h a s t l f h a s m h a s (7)

(is) i f t h i s b e s h e i s t h e s t h f i s t s h i m n i s t h a s t h i s h t s i t h i s t h f l s i s f l s i s (8)

A B C =

Lesson 39

1

______ ______ ______ ______ ______ ______

______ ______ ______ ______ ______ ______

2

1. ____________ 2. ____________ 3. ____________

4. ____________ 5. ____________ 6. ____________

3

her dig digger win winner with

how cast caster fold dinner has

tree slam pack hold thing

4

1. If it is not hot, we will sleep.
2. How did he get so slim?
3. She has a ring on her hand.
4. That cat is slim and sleek.

5

1. ca 2. end 3. im

4. ha 5. ca 6. ee

6

She went to the shop with her list.

She got socks and sheets and sleds and seeds.

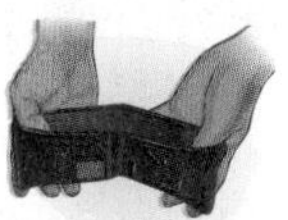

Now she has no cash.

7

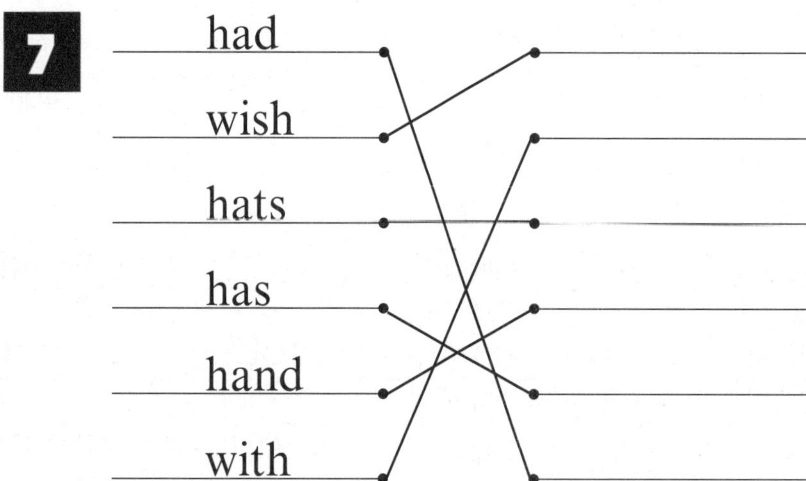

8

(it) fithinsisitifthehisifthieitfheisitifthelilt ithitislitflasitilit (9)

(if) riftisflitifitieiflafifitheflaiflsiflelifilasleifehfiktleifelif (10)

(an) rantanmannamenamanemananemaeoafnamanefoamaname (8)

A | B | C | =

Lesson 40

1

2

1. ______ 2. ______ 3. ______

4. ______ 5. ______ 6. ______

3

pet petting win winner

winning sing singer letter

sheep sleep slop slap slip

4

1. Her pet ram is fat.
2. Will he mend his socks?
3. I am not as sad as I seem.
4. How fast can he go with that cast?

5

1. ack 2. sen 3. li

4. ma 5. end 6. ot

Lesson 40

6

Her dad had a hat.

It did not fit him.

So she got the hat.

It did not fit her.

Now the hat is on her pet pig.

7

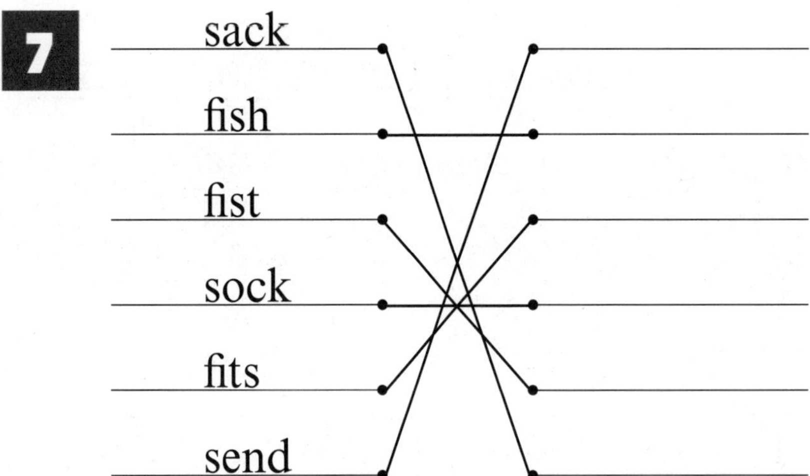

8

(an) tanfranamenamanamenansmeasoamanamenamsaramanman (7)

(and) randtoanhforamdthelandtlkalandthelamdflakahdlandalam (4)

(in) finelsliansimainfielalsmfeinfiemalsfielafnaimainlnlmalim (4)

1

2

1. ______ 2. ______ 3. ______

4. ______ 5. ______ 6. ______

3

fills filling filler fits slam

slap step stem mast master

down winner clam sleds

pots neck fold crash

4

1. I sent her a clock last week.
2. Her dad had a hat that fits.
3. If he is not fast, he will lag.
4. She is petting the sheep and singing.

5

1. ack 2. ick 3. ha

4. ee 5. sa 6. men

6

His truck has no gas.

So he got a can and went for gas.

He did not get gas.

He had no cash.

So this is how he must get up the hill.

7

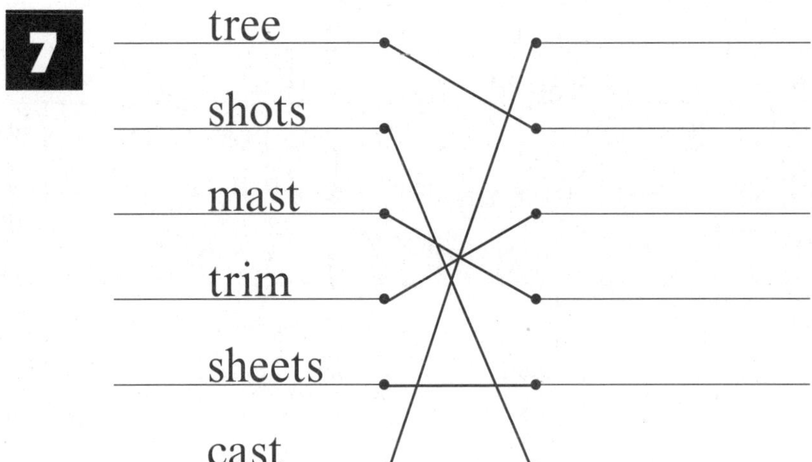

8

(she) thisheforsketheshetohedosdeforshetobemesnethesrefoshe (4)

(shed) thishedheadhadsheddredsderskedtosheddreadshedheadb (4)

(and) grandstandforthebandgothandthemamdtoforandstandabo (6)

A | B | C = [ ]

1

_____ _____ _____ _____ _____ _____

_____ _____ _____ _____ _____ _____

2

1. ________ 2. ________ 3. ________

4. ________ 5. ________ 6. ________

3

rocking up under wishing sending

sender letter slams slaps picks

racks sleep sadder winning mud

4

1. Meet me on the hill.
2. Has he seen his cat this week?
3. That singer will sing at the dinner.
4. The winner got a gold ring.

5

1. ist 2. ash 3. la

4. ack 5. its 6. lo

Lesson 42

6

The hill is steep.

He will run up the hill.

Then he will rest.

He will not sleep.

He will go down that hill and end up in the mud.

7

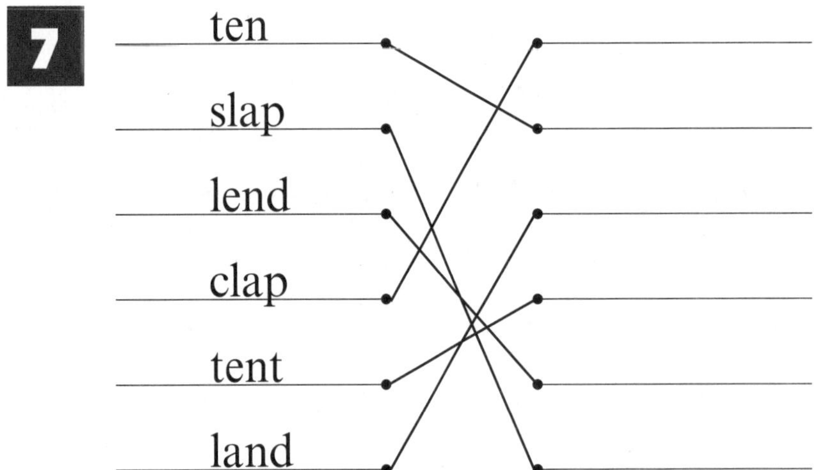

8

(end) trendfenderandindianforendtobendorlendforenhtheemdand (5)

(and) tobstandorlandontothesandadneamdnflanhltklandlaskeand (5)

(the) forthisistheendofthissheetandtheenditistheseadetlsathaim (3)

A | B | C | = |

Lesson 43

1

______ ______ ______ ______ ______ ______

______ ______ ______ ______ ______ ______

2

1. ________ 2. ________

3. ________ 4. ________

5. ________ 6. ________

7. ________ 8. ________

3

1. ha
2. end
3. ack
4. pi
5. fa
6. ish

4

sick

pots

went

last

send

ships

5

1. She has a cast on her leg.
2. Is his pet sheep sick?
3. How can she sleep in the sand?
4. This is a fast sled.
5. Send me the clock this week.
6. I get sadder and sadder when she sings.
7. How will we get dinner on this ship?
8. I wish I had ten cents.

6

We fill pots with clams.

We fit lids on the pots.

We can get the pots hot.

That is how we fix a clam dish.

A B C =

1

_____ _____ _____ _____ _____ _____

_____ _____ _____ _____ _____ _____

2

1. ________ 2. ________ 3. ________

4. ________ 5. ________ 6. ________

3

clam slam mend street for

handing lending clapping rug then

them under than get crash corn

4

1. The old man fell on the dock and got wet.
2. She will fish or sing.
3. Stop filling that gas can with sand.
4. No man will rent that shack.

5

1. ha 2. ma 3. se

4. eets 5. men 6. and

6

He will get up and dig sand.

Then he will run ten laps on the track.

Then he will cut down six trees and sleep for a week.

7

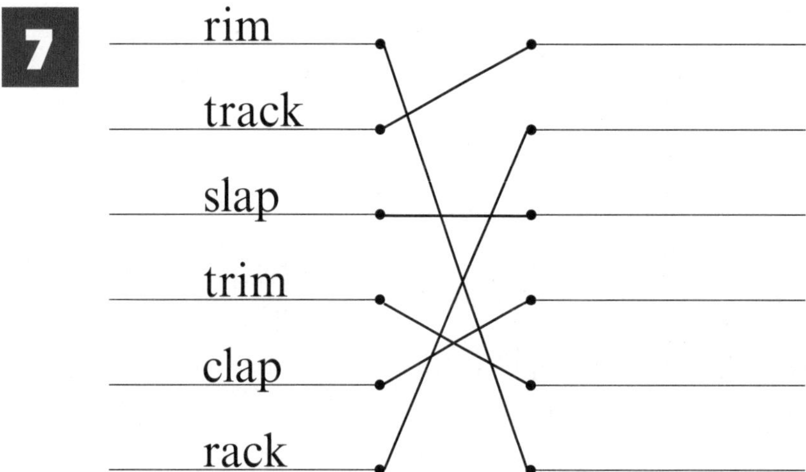

8

(on) frontandontheendomfromtonthalskehfonaofmsoaienfonao (5)

(an) fantanfannisthoamaoaonaosdfiansodifoiasmanasdomasan (6)

(end) bendtothendslendtheioandoelasdkandelkfendaoendlakdne (5)

A | B | C | =

Lesson 45

1

______ ______ ______ ______ ______ ______

______ ______ ______ ______ ______ ______

2

1. ____________ 2. ____________ 3. ____________

4. ____________ 5. ____________ 6. ____________

3

sleep rip grip trip slip he

be sander picker clams got

get wishing horn master ringing

4

1. His socks fit, but his hat is big.
2. She will sing for the class.
3. That man did not land in the sand.
4. She is trim and fast.

5

1. im 2. ts 3. nd

4. cks 5. hi 6. so

Lesson 45

6

She told him to sell the clock.

He went to a shop to sell the clock.

Now he has no clock and no cash.

But he has 3 cats.

7

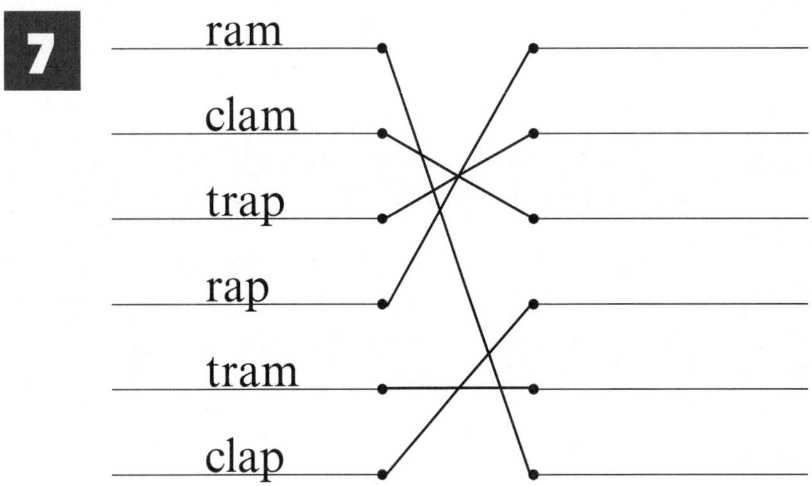

8

(the) freethesheandhethetretneaksthelaskfuethealstheislfiethe (6)

(then) fortothenshelasdkethenasdfkltdentlkathenasdthandlkaft (3)

(end) tothesendlaklsdkendlkaskandflkethendltlkehiasdlendlak (4)

A | B | C =

1

_____ _____ _____ _____ _____ _____

_____ _____ _____ _____ _____ _____

2

1. ________ 2. ________ 3. ________

4. ________ 5. ________ 6. ________

3

trim grim grip green hold

grass class clock trip slip

sleep sheep ship horn sending

so born cot colt sold for

4

1. I am not a big winner.

2. He will lend us his tent.

3. When can I meet that man?

4. We will clap if she sings well.

5

1. st 2. ts 3. ha

4. ot 5. si 6. en

6

That clock is running fast.

It is set for 8.

But it will ring when it is 4.

A man will get up when the clock rings.

But he will not be glad.

7

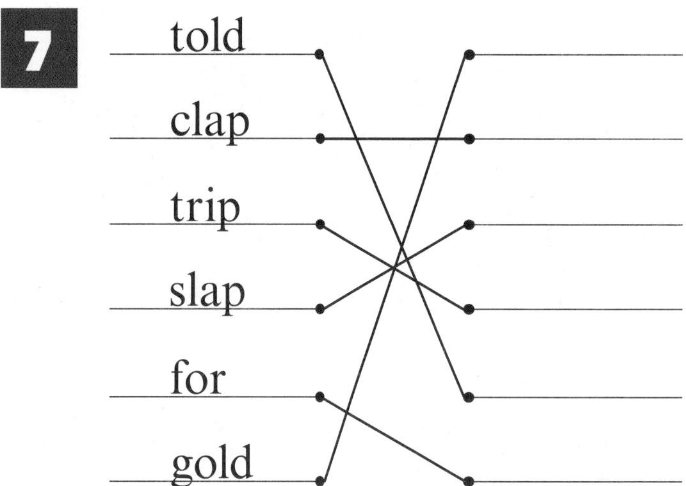

8

(on) tonfomeunemaoneaoemaoenfaoaoneoacnaoencneonoeoaom (4)

(no) tobeonaonoaoaoemaofmanoaoemanofamaofnoaoeaonocane (5)

(ant) rantandthelandamantlalkekfantlalfkehakdlecldaantlekanha (4)

1

_____ _____ _____ _____ _____ _____

_____ _____ _____ _____ _____ _____

2

1. _____ 2. _____ 3. _____

4. _____ 5. _____ 6. _____

3

yell finger sadder master fishing

sled slid bell sander sender

gold mud flaps letter

4

1. We met her at the creek.
2. Is she swimming in the pond?
3. When will the bell ring?
4. She had dinner with us last week.

5

1. ee 2. fa 3. ug

4. co 5. old 6. li

6

We will go fishing.

A big fish is in the creek.

If we get that fish, we will pop it in a pan.

Then we will have a big fish for dinner.

7

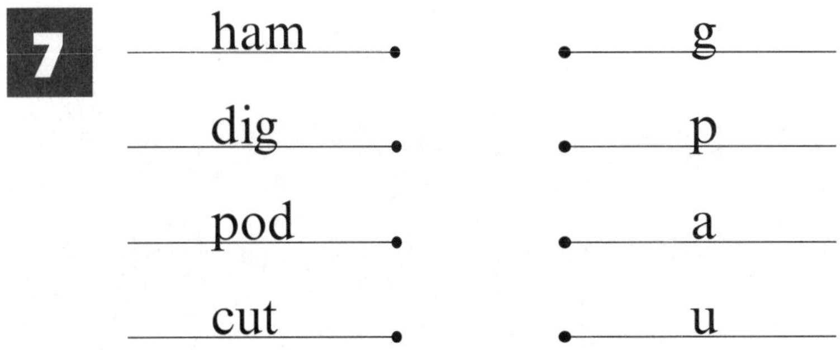

8

has	iashashadohidhasisfisfashachasthisishishashodhadhasfas	5
hand	landhandhadfadfanhandsandstandhandlandfanlantahand	4
no	notoronnoaninontonanotormormonocninanonishonarono	7

A | B | C =

1

____ ____ ____ ____ ____ ____

____ ____ ____ ____ ____ ____

2

1. ______ **2.** ______ **3.** ______

4. ______ **5.** ______ **6.** ______

7. ______ **8.** ______

3

1. lo **2.** ca **3.** end

4. eep **5.** ip **6.** or

4

sock •	• a
clap •	• m
will •	• k
must •	• i

Lesson 48

5

1. The black colt will trot on the track.

2. Her hat fits, but her wig is big.

3. The class will end with a test.

4. The bell will ring for dinner.

5. The flag is old and torn.

6. The fox is running up the steep hill.

7. Send him six green sheets.

6

She will lend us a big tent.

We will go on a trip.

We will swim in the pond.

Then we will set up the tent on a hill.

A | B | C | = |

Lesson 49

1

______ ______ ______ ______ ______ ______

______ ______ ______ ______ ______ ______

2

1. ________ 2. ________ 3. ________

4. ________ 5. ________ 6. ________

7. ________ 8. ________

3

1. se 2. ack 3. ut

4. orn 5. pe 6. ip

4

but •	• i
yes •	• f
dig •	• s
for •	• u

Lesson
49

5

1. How can we fix the truck?

2. Her cat is sleeping in her bed.

3. The swimming class went well.

4. See me sleep in the green grass.

5. Keep sending me happy letters.

6. Now I will cut down six trees.

7. When can we swim at the creek?

8. She left us and got on the bus.

6

A ram was sick.

Six sheep sent him a greeting.

The sheep sent him a big dinner and a gift.

Now he is happy, but he is still sick.

A | B | C =

1

____ ____ ____ ____ ____ ____

____ ____ ____ ____ ____ ____

2

1. ________ 2. ________ 3. ________

4. ________ 5. ________ 6. ________

3

pits under wishing corn morning

fills her pecks peeks street

grass greets sled club lasting

4

1. How can he sleep when we sing?

2. If she is sick, I will send her a greeting.

3. When will she meet us for dinner?

4. The math class did not go well.

5

1. b 2. mu 3. fo

4. ip 5. se 6. ag

6

An ant sat in wet sand.

A man dug in that sand for clams.

The man got 37 clams and 1 wet ant.

That ant and the man had a clam dinner.

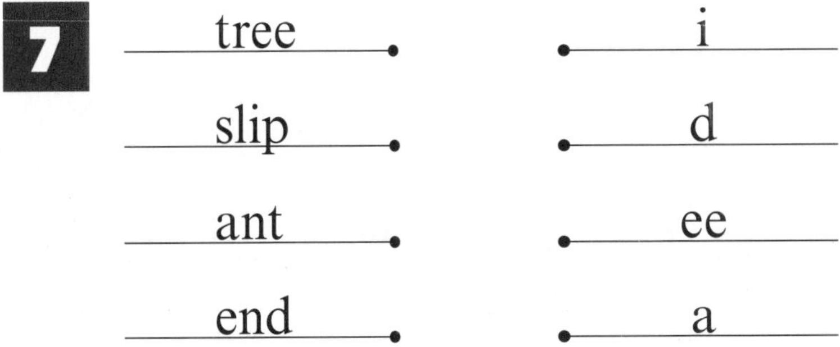

8

(us) upasisusunsusuorunusasishishusfussunisasupunusnsasisn (6)

(send) endsnedesentsendendsentsemdthensendrendsentsenderan (3)

(or) foronusoftooronnorfrontoforomsonsoreformostlonortron (7)

A B C =

1

2

1. ______ 2. ______ 3. ______

4. ______ 5. ______ 6. ______

7. ______

3

best west path felt

cold corn drop drip black

greets club box happy

4

1. She trots faster than the sheep.

2. How can ten men fit in that tent?

3. When they met, they felt happy.

4. When will they stop sending me letters?

Lesson 51

5

1. sl ______ 2. wh ______

3. la ______ 4. ru ______

5. an ______ 6. eep ______

6

The sun was hot.

A pig went on a dusty path.

A cat was in a tree.

It was not hot in the tree.

But a pig can not go up a tree.

So the pig got in the mud.

Now the pig is happy.

7

track •	• e
lend •	• ck
slid •	• p
shop •	• i

8

(the) thatthehishethefreehethethisthatthemthanthethashehethe (6)

(and) antandendsandfendtrandlendantamdsamtsardandlondtrant (4)

(she) seepsheetseemshoresheshareshadsheenshashoasheshcseem (4)

A | B | C =

Lesson 52

1

___ ___ ___ ___ ___ ___

___ ___ ___ ___ ___ ___

2

1. ________ 2. ________ 3. ________

4. ________ 5. ________ 6. ________

7. ________

3

gripping shops chops bust under

peeks dusty lands truck tent laps

clapping clipping morning box mold

4

1. They will lock the shed in the morning.

2. Then she told me how happy she was.

3. That bug was green and black.

4. Did she go to the store yet?

5. How did that clock get a dent in it?

Lesson
52

5

1. sl 2. mu 3. co

4. im 5. la 6. eep

6

Ten men got in a truck.

They went to the creek and set up a tent.

How can ten men fit in the tent?

They can not. 4 men will sleep in the tent.

2 men will sleep under a tree.

4 men will sleep in the truck.

7

pets •	• d
and •	• t
clam •	• l
rubs •	• b

8

(then) tenhenthenthemhemtenhenthenthethatththenthethanthen (4)

(he) henhathehashishihohehahentenmenfencehenthansahahe (6)

(had) hashathashadhavehashedheadhashhadhamfadsadhadmad (3)

A | B | C | = |

Lesson 53

1

_____ _____ _____ _____ _____ _____

_____ _____ _____ _____ _____ _____

2

1. _____ 2. _____ 3. _____

4. _____ 5. _____ 6. _____

7. _____

3

1. amp 2. olt 3. s

4. sl 5. ey 6. ye

4

short •	• ch
sold •	• th
much •	• or
bath •	• ol

5

1. He said, "I will go to the store."

2. She told him, "Go rent a truck."

3. They said, "We had fun on the trip."

6

1. Next week, we will plant six seeds.

2. Send me a better letter.

3. On the trip, I got sick.

4. For lunch, they had fish and chips.

7

She told him, "Let us go on a clipper ship."

But he had no cash. And she had no cash.

He said, "We will pan for gold."

So they went to the hills. They got gold.

Then they went on that clipper ship.

A B C =

Lesson 54

1

2

1. ______ 2. ______ 3. ______

4. ______ 5. ______ 6. ______

7. ______

3

chip	sand	bent	rents	big	
bug	gripping	help	need	they	
silly	for	now	mats	slug	rag

4

1. He said, "I will win the meet."
2. She said, "Fix the casters on that bed."
3. The clock was running faster.
4. We went and sat under the tree.
5. If we rent a truck, we can go on a trip.

Lesson 54

5

1. co 2. im 3. sa

4. t 5. nd 6. d

6

The dog was wet and muddy. Ted said, "That dog needs a bath." Ann said, "Get a rag." Ted did that. Then he said, "I will fill the tub." So the dog got a bath. But Ann and Ted got wet and muddy.

7

land	i
clip	t
flaps	d
step	o
on	f

8

(be) m e h e b e t h e b e s e h e s h e t h e t h a t b e o r b a b y b o y b y b e b u m t h e d e n e (4)

(up) u p o r u g f o r u p o n t h e h u g o t h e r u p u f u h e u y r u g t o u p t h e d u d h u g (4)

(when) t h e n w h e n w h o t h a t t h a n w h a t w h e n w h e r e w h e n w h a n t h e w e n h n (3)

A | B | C | =

1

2

1. ________ 2. ________ 3. ________

4. ________ 5. ________ 6. ________

3

wheel well bump clamp bold

yet self shelf bath such felt

morning dripping muddy next better

4

1. On the next morning, he felt happy.

2. She said, "Was the cat sleeping under the bed?"

3. We do not sit in wet sand.

4. Help that man lift this box.

5. If the sheet is torn, we will mend it.

6. At last, she got socks that fit.

Lesson 55

5

1. le 2. amp 3. en

4. eep 5. eep 6. em

6

A horse met a sheep. The horse said, “I can trot faster than a sheep.” The sheep got mad. Then the horse said, “And I can swim faster than a sheep.” The sheep said, “But I can do this better than a horse.” The sheep went to sleep.

7

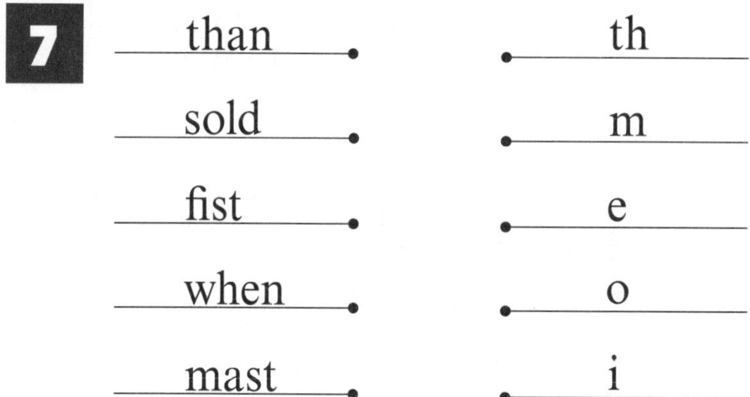

8

(when) thenwhenwhowhenthatwhatthenwhentobeenwhemthewen (3)

(if) tifthisifistobeitcandoidinanaforiftoisitihifitisaninifina (5)

(she) theshehebefreeshetobehemetheshethishasteshethemeshef (5)

1

2

1. ______ 2. ______ 3. ______

4. ______ 5. ______ 6. ______

7. ______

3

next drops wet greets champs

dump went slips much

mister folding clock under greeting

4

1. Go to the flag and stand still.
2. The tracks led to the shack next to the hill.
3. If she can dig, she can plant this tree.
4. Was she picking up jam at the store?
5. How much cash do they need?

Lesson 56

5

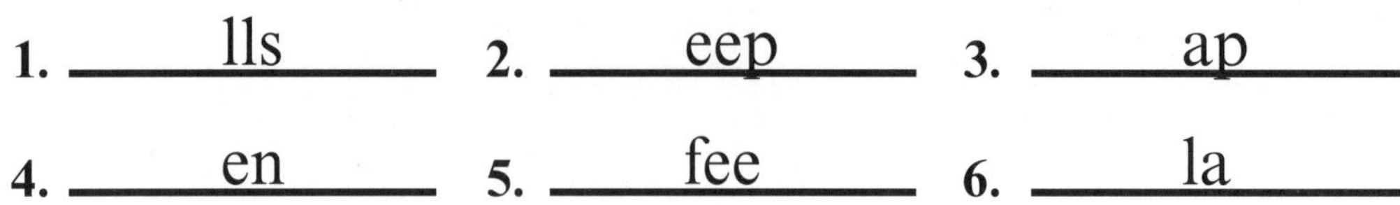

1. lls
2. eep
3. ap
4. en
5. fee
6. la

6

Ann was a winner on the track. And she was the best singer in town. She said to her self, "I need cash. I can get a job running or a job singing." She got the best job. She is the singer at track meets, and she is glad.

7

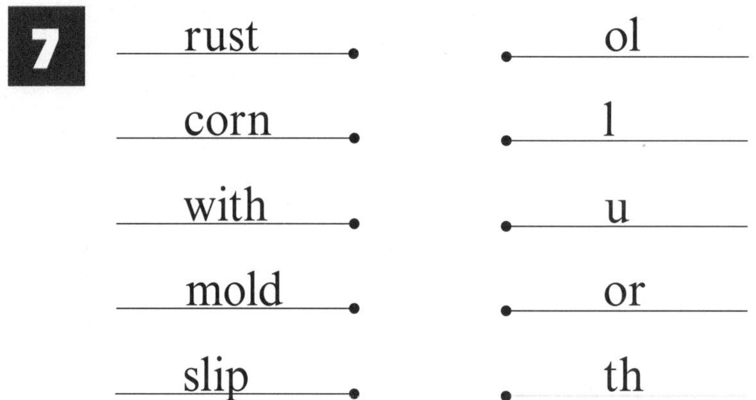

rust
corn
with
mold
slip
ol
l
u
or
th

8

(not) tonornotnobnotomotnofnodnotnornodnofnobnotontoreorn (4)

(be) mehefeebeteethebeheshethebemebathebetmetmenbanbeam (5)

(an) tanconfromamanoninanamonomiminantinamantmennantan (7)

A B C =

Lesson 57

1

_____ _____ _____ _____ _____ _____

_____ _____ _____ _____ _____ _____

2

1. ________ 2. ________ 3. ________

4. ________ 5. ________ 6. ________

7. ________

3

clash lift west lunch singer

flip slipping rust crust north

licks winning jumps champ clamp

4

1. He told me, "Do not go to class."

2. How steep is that hill?

3. We must plant more corn seeds.

4. Do they need help with that horse?

5. How fast can she cut the grass?

6. She said, "Do not set that pen on the desk."

Lesson 57

5

1. fi 2. th 3. en

4. ca 5. we 6. ip

6

Bud and Al went on a trip. Al said, "We will stop for lunch." They sat on a hill next to the pond. They did not see that the hill was an ant hill. The ants got cold cuts and chips. Al got ants in his pants.

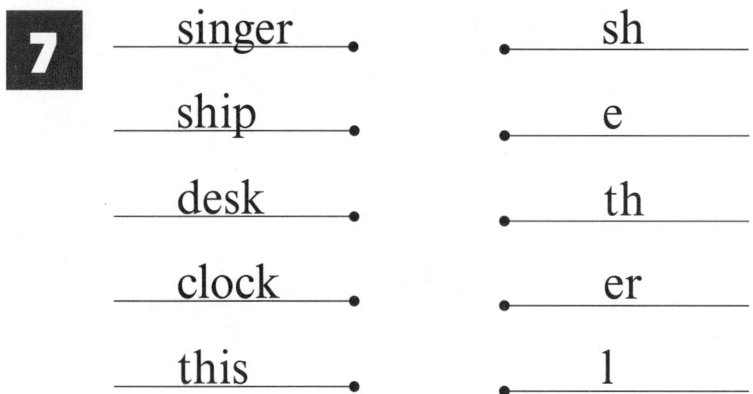

7
singer
ship
desk
clock
this
sh
e
th
er
l

8

(in) oninanmantantindandimdindonaninanonmanmadmidtinfan (5)

(it) ifitihitthistoifihnlittlerisitinatoranratfantinasitisifitisan (6)

(was) sawcandowaswantthatwhatwhasawmanwasthatwantwaswa (3)

A B C =

1

_____ _____ _____ _____ _____ _____

_____ _____ _____ _____ _____ _____

2

1. ________ 2. ________ 3. ________

4. ________ 5. ________ 6. ________

7. ________ 8. ________

3

rest winning pants clash rushing

better telling thing path colt

ring swimmer sacks bother much

4

1. Did you see six black bugs under the rug?

2. Now it is sunny, so we can swim.

3. Go to the next class as fast as you can.

4. What do they see on the bus?

5. They said, "We will plant the last of the seeds."

Lesson 58

5

1. ca 2. hi 3. im

4. ip 5. ro 6. ab

6

He said, "We must get a gift for Pam." She said, "We can get her a green frog or a pet fish." "No," he said. "We will get her a black cat or a big horse." She said, "That is silly. We can not get her a horse." So they got her a colt.

7

trap	ee
short	ap
beet	g
fold	ol
dents	nt
go	or

8

(chip) shipchipchopchapchipchinchanshipchimchapchopchipchi (3)

(was) sawantascanwasseewastetobeasintoforwashaswawatwas (4)

(no) oninanoeisantoaienoaneoafaioeansfmenafmenoaiemfon (3)

A B C =

Lesson 59

1

______ ______ ______ ______ ______ ______

______ ______ ______ ______ ______ ______

2

1. ____________ **2.** ____________ **3.** ____________

4. ____________ **5.** ____________ **6.** ____________

7. ____________ **8.** ____________

3

things runs clips bother

lunch yells deep desk bolt

swing rent check pinning self

4

1. If he is happy, he will slap us on the back.

2. Do you need to go to town?

3. See that horse run on a dusty path.

4. Do you smell the jam?

5. What do you do in the morning?

6. "Hand me the pen," she said.

7. What gift was she wishing for?

5

1. dr 2. ee 3. ma

4. ink 5. le 6. op

7. fi

6

He told me how to get to the best store in town. He told me to go left at the gift shop and go north. He said, "Then you will go six blocks to the west." He said, "Then go up the hill and down the next street." Do you think I got to the store? No. I got lost.

7

sleep	nt
under	u
big	er
dug	b
sent	ee
trip	ip

8

(when) thenthanwhenwhattheythanwhanwhenthethiswhatwhentot (3)

(to) itistoofhotheonethletoshflaofhsthotatontoforisthefotioto (5)

(has) hishamhashimherhashcantrashishisforhashamandhisfasto (3)

A | B | C | =

1

2

1. ______ 2. ______ 3. ______

4. ______ 5. ______ 6. ______

7. ______ 8. ______

3

feels letters blush crush jelly

funny greeting lunch mold

ringing next west store very

4

1. He said, "What can I do so that you will feel better?"
2. What was she picking on top of the hill?
3. They had lots of desks in the class.
4. She said, "Stand still or you will slip."
5. What will you get when you go to the store?

Lesson 60

5

1. am 2. dr 3. an

4. ho 5. eeps 6. we

6

We had a clock that did not run. We went to a clock fixer and said, “Can you fix this clock?” He said, “Yes, I can get it to run.” The next morning, we went back to pick up the clock. The old man held up the clock. He said, “I stuck legs on the clock. Now it will run.”

7

chop	u
then	th
jam	sh
ship	ch
fork	or
but	a

8

(to) forothotoformhastobeholdcoldorhastobeinthetoitoftheof (5)

(ship) shifthishipintoshoresirshinerohtheshipishapelyshipshop (3)

(was) sawthewhatwashetherehasmastobenwasawaythenasmashe (2)

A | B | C =

1

______ ______ ______ ______ ______ ______

______ ______ ______ ______ ______ ______

2

1. ______ 2. ______ 3. ______

4. ______ 5. ______ 6. ______

7. ______

3

1. ju 2. eck 3. sho

4. ell 5. cla 6. re

4

chip •	• x
horn •	• a
jump •	• r
was •	• u
next •	• i

5

1. Do you think we can go swimming if it gets sunny?

2. Check with the man at the desk.

3. What did they do after dinner?

4. Did she keep her hands on the wheel?

5. You can not do math as well as I can.

6

An old truck did not stop well. Sandy got in the truck and went to the top of a steep hill. Then she went down the hill faster and faster. She said, “I do not think I can stop this truck.” A pond was at the end of the street. Now Sandy is sitting in a wet truck with six frogs.

A | B | C | =

Lesson 62

1

2

1. ______ 2. ______ 3. ______

4. ______ 5. ______ 6. ______

7. ______ 8. ______

3

dust very big dig bust buns

left such butter batter sender

folder lucky feeling crush flags

4

1. How did so much dust get on the plants?

2. She said, “We can get more chips at the store.”

3. You left lots of things on her desk.

4. What did she do when she felt bad?

5. After dinner, we will sit on the swing.

5

1. op 2. th 3. ha

4. st 5. nt 6. d

6

Ann went to the bun shop with her mixer. She said, "With this batter mixer, I can fix the best batter." "No," the men said. "We fix the best batter. It has the best butter." She said, "Mix the best butter with this batter mixer." So they did. They got the best buns in town.

7

ship	ck
sold	ch
chip	ee
tubs	sh
locks	u
creek	ol

8

(end) lendthandhenhandcanendsentforlendthenhasadtoends (4)

(much) suchgoodmuchcanshouldmochormuchtouchatmuchhut (3)

(on) tonforaninamonemaosoemaosnaoeoonasinanimonoma (4)

1

______ ______ ______ ______ ______ ______

______ ______ ______ ______ ______ ______

2

1. ______ 2. ______ 3. ______

4. ______ 5. ______ 6. ______

7. ______ 8. ______

3

docks hammer champ chopping shopping

bunch sweet very junk butter

bother crush held stuck swinging

4

1. When will we get to the top of the hill?

2. What will we fix for dinner?

3. How well do you sleep in this tent?

4. That jam is very red and sweet.

5. They had to do the planting in the spring.

6. She was yelling, "Stop that bus."

Lesson 63

5

1. eep 2. t 3. l

4. h 5. w 6. b

6

Her mom told her, "The street is slick. So do not go on it." But she went in the street with her slippers. The slippers did not grip the street. She fell on her back. Her mom said, "I told you it was slick." She said, "Yes, I just went slipping in slippers."

7

much	or
tells	m
slams	g
lunch	ll
form	a
bugs	l

8

(chop) shopthechoptheposhipchipchopshipchopshopchinshinc (3)

(do) todoofhothedomeisotopordoorcandoitorfrotheedtodow (5)

(this) thisishisshipasthisisthatornotthinforthesthisasthinhis (3)

A B C =

1

2

1. ______ 2. ______ 3. ______

4. ______ 5. ______ 6. ______

7. ______ 8. ______

3

tub quit mixer which stuck

vest sitting checks vet shops

lucky chip shelf tell till skunk

4

1. If I ask, he will lend me his vest.

2. You can chop lots of nuts with that mixer.

3. Which cat sat on this desk?

4. His mom said, "Stop sitting on that stump."

5. It was sunny on top of this hill.

5

1. d 2. m 3. h

4. p 5. p 6. p

6

After lunch, Pam and her dad went to the vet with a sick frog. They sat down next to a man that had a skunk. Pam said to the man, “Can I pet that skunk?” The man said, “Do not bother this skunk. Or you will smell a big stink.” Just then, the frog went hop, hop. And what do you think that skunk did?

7

tipping	tt
better	j
singer	pp
just	er
clocks	ch
such	cks

8

(much) s u c h m u c h t o u c h h u t c h s u c h m u c h m i c h o r s i c k m o c t o u c h m u c h (3)

(then) w h e n t h e n h e n t h a n t h a t w h e n w h a t t h e n a s t h e m o r t h a n t h e n t h e 

(bad) h a d t o s a d o f b a d t h e s a d b a d h a d h a t b a t c a n h a d b a d h a t c a n b a n (3)

A B C =

1

_____ _____ _____ _____ _____ _____ _____

_____ _____ _____ _____ _____ _____ _____

2

1. ________ **2.** ________ **3.** ________

4. ________ **5.** ________ **6.** ________

7. ________ **8.** ________

3

very self green clips block

glass slipper stump shell path

clamp quick mister dust flips

4

1. What did she do with the truck?

2. Her dad told her, "Send me a letter."

3. You will feel happy when that horse wins.

4. Which slippers will fit on this shelf?

5. The old man said, "That sink is not for drinking."

6. Will you ask her how much the rent is?

Lesson 65

5

1. ee 2. f 3. m

4. d 5. p 6. p

7. ca

6

A green frog was in a bath tub. A red bug said, "Can I get in the tub with you?" "No," the frog said. "This tub is for me." The bug said, "But I need a bath." The frog said, "Go hop in the sink." That is what the bug did. It went for a swim in the sink.

7

still	ck
bold	st
sending	m
truck	b
slaps	ing
trim	a

8

(do) todoofthetomodoefoaofodoaoeofmdogoadleidohdowohodo (7)

(bad) sadhadbadcaddadasanaddfadbadsadtheladhadasadbadcad (3)

(was) sawasasawarcancawarmasthatwasawforwashingthewasitfa (4)

Name: ______________________ Date: ____________

1

___ ___ ___ ___ ___ ___ ___ ___

___ ___ ___ ___ ___ ___ ___ ___

Number of errors [ ] P F

2

1. ____________ 2. ____________ 3. ____________

4. ____________ 5. ____________ 6. ____________

Number of errors [ ] P F

3

1. co 2. ca 3. ru

4. eets 5. ip 6. fi

Number of errors [ ] P F

4

ship •	• ck
locks •	• ch
chip •	• ee
creek •	• sh

Number of errors [ ] P F

Mastery Test 15

5

(when) thenwhenwhowhenthatthenwhentowhenwemthewhenhwenn

(if) tifthisifistibeitcafidpifinanaforiftoifitihifitisintninifiithi

Number of errors ☐ P F

6

funny letter horse happy sold torn

Number of errors ☐ P F

7

mast went gift help rocks

hits dust seeds rags end

Number of errors ☐ P F

8

flag crack drip crust clock

grim black street sling green

Number of errors ☐ P F

9

them mash when teeth wheel with

Number of errors ☐ P F

10

to said you do of was

Number of errors ☐ P F

11 and **12**

Ann was a winner on the track.

And she was the best singer in town.

She said to her self, "I need cash.

I can get a job running or a job singing."

She got the best job.

She is a singer at track meets, and she is glad.

13

Record student's answers here.

1. *What are the two things that Ann could do well?*

2. *Tell me what Ann said to herself.*

3. *Why is that the best job for her?*

Number of errors ☐ P F